Adéwálé Májà-Pearce is one of Nigeria's leading public intellectuals. He is the author of two memoirs, *In My Father's Country* and *The House My Father Built*. His writing regularly appears in the *New York Times*, *London Review of Books*, and *Times Literary Supplement*.

**SOUTHERN
QUESTIONS**

Decolonisation was the major historical process of the twentieth century. Its unfinished projects continue to shape our present. The defeat, withdrawal, and reconfiguration of Western colonial power in the postwar decades have affected almost everyone alive today, with stunning unevenness. The Southern Questions series features first-hand accounts – memoirs, novels, pamphlets – written by participants in the drama of decolonisation and its aftermath. Alongside these titles, Southern Questions presents new histories, reportage, and literary criticism devoted to nations, regions, and zones in the South.

Adom Getachew
Thomas Meaney
Series Editors

This Fiction Called Nigeria

The Struggle for Democracy

Adéwálé Májà-Pearce

VERSO

London • New York

First published by Verso 2024
© Adéwálé Májà-Pearce 2024

Large parts of Chapter 1 originally appeared in *The Baffler*,
'Sorrow, Tears and Blood', Issue 57, 3 May 2021.

Some parts of Chapter 2 appeared in *The
Baffler*, 'A Violent Enterprise', 11
May 2022.

Significant portions of Chapter 4 appeared
in the following pieces: *London
Review of Books*, 'Army Arrangement', Vol.
21, No., 7, 1 April 1999; 'Diary: In
Northern Nigeria', 12 December 2002; and
'Where to begin?', 26 April 2018.

1 3 5 7 9 10 8 6 4 2

Verso
UK: 6 Meard Street, London W1F 0EG
US: 388 Atlantic Avenue, Brooklyn, NY 11217
versobooks.com

Verso is the imprint of New Left Books

ISBN-13: 978-1-80429-180-1
ISBN-13: 978-1-80429-182-5 (US EBK)
ISBN-13: 978-1-80429-181-8 (UK EBK)

British Library Cataloguing in Publication Data
A catalogue record for this book is available from the British Library

Library of Congress Cataloging-in-Publication Data

Names: Májà-Pearce, Adéwálé, author.
Title: This fiction called Nigeria : the struggle for democracy /
    Adéwálé Májà-Pearce.
Description: London ; New York : Verso, 2024. | Includes bibliographical
    references.
Identifiers: LCCN 2024014098 (print) | LCCN
2024014099 (ebook) | ISBN
    9781804291801 (paperback) | ISBN
9781804291825 (US ebook) | ISBN
    9781804291818 (UK ebook)
Subjects: LCSH: Democracy--Nigeria. | Nigeria--Politics and government.
Classification: LCC JQ3096 .M35 2024 (print)
| LCC JQ3096 (ebook) | DDC
    320.4669--dc23/eng/20240613
LC record available at https://lccn.loc.gov/2024014098
LC ebook record available at https://lccn.loc.gov/2024014099

Typeset in Sabon by Biblichor Ltd, Scotland
Printed and bound by CPI Group (UK) Ltd, Croydon CR0 4YY

We must choose either champagne for a few or safe drinking water for all.

– Thomas Sankara

To:

Sir (Dr) Adéwálé Adéṣọ́jí Adéèyò, OON (1948–2021), whose generous commission all those years ago forms part of this book;

and

the Civitella Ranieri Foundation, which granted me a fellowship in 2022 that proved decisive for this book, Italy and Nigeria having more in common than one might otherwise suspect. But that is for another book.

Contents

Preface

This book was written against the background of the 2023 elections. By then, we had 'enjoyed' almost a quarter-century of democracy, having previously 'endured' roughly the same under the military. I use quotation marks because, although the population doubled to 220 million in that period (making us the sixth largest nation in the world), it was also the case that a greater number of Nigerians fell into extreme poverty, currently standing at 133 million.[1] Given that most of them are young, it is hardly surprising that they are also becoming increasingly restless in the face of their bleak prospects, as witness the 2020 #EndSARS movement that led to the slaughter of peaceful demonstrators.

Our underlying problem is that we are not really a country in any coherent sense, hence the title. What passes for 'Nigeria' is an amalgam of both world religions (in roughly equal numbers) and over 250 ethnic groups, with often wildly different traditions, all of them arbitrarily yoked together by the British colonial power for its own economic interests.[2] The British themselves knew very well that the

---

1 The population figure in wide use is almost certainly wrong. The actual population might be as low as 120 million, but this is the figure widely used; see Tope Fasua, 'Nigeria's population is a lot less than 200 million', *Premium Times*, 20 March 2023.

2 Perhaps we should call it the English Empire given that the Irish, Scots and Welsh were also colonised ahead of the rest upon which the

predominantly Muslim North and the predominantly Christian South – the deepest and most obvious of our many divides – were as different from each other 'as England is from China', to quote Sir George Goldie, the man most responsible for realising what might just be the world's most complex country, made more so by the imbalance between the ethnicities. Just three of them – Hausa-Fulani in the North, Igbo in the South-east and Yorùbá in the southwest – comprise roughly two-thirds of the total, rendering all the others 'minorities', as they are made to understand whenever they forget themselves.

Indeed, so dominant were these three in their respective areas – and so mistrustful of the others – that the British initially divided the country into three semi-autonomous regions with a weak centre. Even at that, each region threatened at one time or another to secede, both before and after independence in 1960, a series of threats that culminated in civil war seven years later when the Igbo went the distance and declared the Republic of Biafra. Tellingly, the war itself was fought under the vacuous slogan 'To Keep Nigeria One/Is A Task That Must Be Done', which was entirely in keeping with the equally vacuous 1960 UN charter, *On the Granting of Independence to Colonial Countries and People* – 'Any attempt aimed at the partial or total disruption of the national unit and the territorial integrity of a country is incompatible with the purposes and principles of the charter of the United Nations' – that contradicted the same UN's own *Covenant on Human Rights*: 'All peoples and all nations shall have the right of self-determination.' As it happened, both the United States

---

sun seems to be setting ever closer to home post-Brexit. Still, at least we all speak English, which ought to be some sort of solace to those who set store by the supposed past greatness, whatever the cost in human lives.

and the then Soviet Union supported Nigeria (and not just with 'ordinary mouth', as we say), and this at the height of the Cold War with the 1962 Cuban Missile Crisis still fresh in everyone's minds.

In fact, the real reason why the Northern Region didn't want the Eastern Region to secede – and possibly the Western Region along with it – was economic, as the British reminded them. Originally, the Northern Nigeria Protectorate and the Southern Nigeria Protectorate were administered as two different territories but were amalgamated because the 'promising youth' of the former couldn't pay his way and so was betrothed to the 'southern lady of means', enriched first from the proceeds of palm oil and then by the even more lucrative crude that was discovered in commercial quantities in 1956, most of it in the minority areas adjacent to Igbo territory included in the short-lived Republic of Biafra. In many ways, the story of Nigeria is the story of oil, the proceeds of which provided us with 'the chance, clearly within our grasp, to become a medium-rank developed nation in the 20th century', according to Chinua Achebe, the celebrated novelist, instead of which we created a cabal of fabulously wealthy chiefs in what is one of the world's most unequal countries: the five richest men are worth US$29.9bn between them, courtesy of the US$20 trillion stolen from the treasury between 1960 and 2005.[3] Worse yet, it seems their only ambition is to rape girls. Take, for instance, Ahmad Sani Yerima, the former two-term governor of Zamfara State and two-term federal senator who threatened to vie for the 2023 presidency but then didn't put himself forward when the time

---

3 Chinua Achebe, *The Education of a British-Protected Child*, New York: Anchor Books, 2009, 44; *Nigeria: Extreme inequality in numbers*, Oxfam International, 2022.

came. During his tenure as senator, he bought his Egyptian driver's thirteen-year-old daughter as his fourth wife for US$100,000. When it was pointed out that the senate itself had passed the Child Rights Act (which Zamfara had refused to ratify under his watch), he retorted, 'History tells us that the Prophet Muhammad did marry a young girl as well. I have not contravened any law.' It should be said in this context that Nigerian legislators pay themselves more than their Swedish counterparts because, as the outgoing leader of the House of Representatives once told me, Nigerian lawmakers have more mouths to feed than their 'developed' counterparts, itself the consequence of an unproductive economy in which politics is the only route to wealth. Just recently, this same No. 4 citizen flew 100 guests to Dubai to celebrate his mother's ninetieth birthday, perhaps because there was nowhere expensive enough to cater to his demanding dependants in the country he purports to legislate for.

So why do we, the 'people', the 'masses', tolerate such levels of obscenity? Consider that the victor in the 2023 presidential election, Bọlá Ahmed Tinúbú, claims to be a descendant of the most successful indigenous slave trader in nineteenth-century Lagos, after whom a prominent downtown square is named. It says something about our warped or perhaps non-existent sense of the history no longer taught in our public schools that nobody has yet suggested renaming it, perhaps for fear of drawing attention to our complicity in selling our brothers and sisters to the White Man anchored off the malaria-infested coast. Even more humiliating (although shame is necessarily not among Tinúbú's attributes), the descendants of the slave trader have themselves disowned him; but then Tinúbú has lied about many things, including his name, age, place of birth and qualifications, such is the calibre of the person who would seek to rule us. As we shall see in due course, he is also a thug, but then that is the nature of our politics. Not that Atiku Abubakar, the second of the three leading hopefuls in the run-up to election day, was much better. The third, Peter Obi, was something of a phenomenon because of the way he was unexpectedly taken up by the youths in order to bring about the change they persistently craved, with no demand on his part to be paid for services rendered. This has never happened before and looked to many to be the miracle that all but the chiefs and emirs fervently pray for in our myriad churches and mosques, Nigerians being a worshipful people.

Without such change the country will disintegrate of its own accord. Indeed, it is doing so as I write, what with the Islamic fundamentalists, cattle-rearing bandits and kidnappers who have rendered travel by road and rail unsafe in any part of the country since 2019. But there is a deeper, existential sense in which we have lost our way, recognised as such by the same Achebe, deemed the 'father of African literature' on account of *Things Fall Apart*. Both at the beginning and the end of his illustrious career, which concluded with the publication of *There Was a Country*, he obsessed over whether he had committed a 'dreadful betrayal' of his mother tongue and therefore his culture by writing in the language of the colonial master. But at least he spelt his name correctly. Not so the English-language Yorùbá writers who eschew the diacritics or accents with special characters that are the distinctive feature of a language in which vowels are of greater importance than consonants and tones are of greater importance than vowels.[4] This obviously simplifies matters for the audience

---

4 I am also guilty of this because I was gifted a Yorùbá name but not the language, for reasons inherent in what follows.

their work is primarily aimed at, a readership under the influence of what Fẹlá Aníkúlápó Kútì, the legendary Afrobeat musician dubbed 'colo-mentality': the anxiety to be understood by others ahead of ourselves. As Wọlé Ṣóyínká, the 1986 Nobel laureate, once remarked, 'To go back and say that you will write only in your local language is, for me, very defeatist ... Why should I speak only to the Yoruba alone?'[5]

But perhaps speaking 'only to the Yoruba alone' is the whole point. Moreover, for a playwright especially, there was already a long tradition of Yorùbá folk opera which had thrived in its modern form since the late nineteenth century:

> As early as 1882, a correspondent of the *Lagos Observer* had made a strong plea for discarding 'borrowed plumes' in the form of European ... literature in favour of 'the legends connected with our own ancestors as handed down to us by tradition'. By the turn of the century, the African amateur dramatists, mainly drawn from the ranks of the secessionist churches, were performing works mainly on local themes and in the native language – Yoruba.[6]

The real innovator was Hubert Ògúndé, who led the revival of travelling theatre in the 1940s and was celebrated as such by a visiting oyibo (white) man, who wrote in the *Daily Service* newspaper:

---

5 Nii K. Bentsi-Enchill, 'Wole Soyinka in Stockholm', in *Conversations with Wole Soyinka*, ed. Biodun Jeyifo, Jackson: University Press of Mississippi, 2001, 142. When quoting Yorùbá names from primary sources I obviously use the spelling the writers themselves use.

6 Oyekan Owomoyela, *Folklore and Yoruba Theater*, Bloomington: Indiana University Press, 1971, 31.

Since my arrival in this country, I have seen many African plays and operas ... but I had the greatest surprise of my life when I attended the rehearsal of the African opera entitled Mr Devil's Money by the African Music Research Party of Hubert Ogunde ... scheduled to be staged at the Glover Hall on Monday, May 6, 1946.

The theme is based on an old African story depicting the theme of 'here and after' of a man who signed a pact with an evil spirit in order to be wealthy. To see the cast rehearsing the Opera dances, to hear the cheap Native drums supplying the music with precision without any mechanical aid, the clapping of hands, and the high standard of discipline maintained throughout is to think one is back at a London theatre. The singing is excellent. Dance formations, lightings and the stage setting are concrete proofs that the African is no more behind as many people think.[7]

As an editorial in the same newspaper remarked, 'Our progress as a country does not depend solely on the number of so-called enlightened politicians but on the development of as many aspects of our national life as possible. We must advance on all points – in politics, in education, in art and in poetry – if we are to prevent a lopsided development.'[8] And yet, within four years of independence Ògúndé was banned from performing following the popularity of his play *Yorùbá Ronu/Yorùbá Think*, which toured the towns and villages criticizing the Yorùbá leadership for promoting internal divisions in service of their own selfish motives. (His immediate response was another play, *Òtító Korò/*

---

7   Quoted in Ebun Clark, 'Ogunde Theatre: The Rise of Contemporary Theatre in Nigeria', in *Drama and Theatre in Nigeria: A Critical Source Book*, ed. Yemi Ogunbiyi, Lagos: Nigeria Magazine, 1981, 296.

8   Ibid.

Truth Is Bitter.) Ironically, the person responsible for the ban, Chief S. L. Akíntọ́lá, had been editor of the same *Daily Service* (which at the time promoted the same Ògúndé) but was now premier of the Western Region (of which more anon) and seemingly hell-bent on 'a lopsided development' in which education, art and poetry had no place. A further irony is that Ògúndé had previously suffered in like manner under the colonial government when two of his plays – *Strike Hunger* and *Bread and Bullet* – were similarly banned in the 1940s, thus demonstrating early on the continuity between colonial and post-colonial politics. Not that any of this stopped either Ògúndé or the others who wrote only in Yorùbá – over a hundred by the 1970s, according to one source – from retaining the adulation of a language group now put at 40 million, as the irrepressible German impresario Ulli Beier recorded when yet another practitioner, E. K. Ògunmọlá, returned to the stage in 1972 following a protracted illness:

> It was an incredible event. The nightclub, which sometimes serves as a theatre for Yoruba Operas, could normally hold perhaps three hundred people, but on this occasion there must have been at least a thousand, tightly packed, filling out every square inch . . . and crowding the street outside. The excitement and the noise were incredible.[9]

Meanwhile, to keep 'the people' distracted, the chiefs we allow to lord it over us cynically evoke ethnic and religious sentiment even as they 'chop and clean mouth' in the National Assembly, all in their traditional attire, Nigerian men verging on the peacock, a dandyism which unites all

---

9 Ulli Beier, 'E. K. Ogunmola: A Personal Memoir', in *Drama and Theatre in Nigeria*, ed. Ogunbiyi, 330–1.

the otherwise disparate ethnic groups, and which at least makes the brigandage a colourful affair. However, should 'the masses' become restless with their antics, as they show increasing signs of doing, out comes the military to crush peaceful demonstrators asking, for instance, that the police desist from killing young men as suspected scammers simply because they happen to be driving flashy cars. But then Nigeria was designed as a militarised state by the colonial 'master' to whom we continue to pay obeisance, whatever the noises about the democracy that has been tested once again, which was why said masters' hand-maidens dutifully reported to Chatham House in London a month before the 2023 vote, a contest that nobody expected to be peaceful, free or fair; but whether the great army of youths could pull off what would have amounted to a peaceful revolution by electing Peter Obi for no other reason than that they wanted competent government – or, at least, the beginnings of it – was the first challenge.

The second challenge was to convene a genuinely sovereign national conference where all the different interest groups – ethnic, linguistic, religious – would sit down together and decide whether they even want to stay together and, if so, how. This would be the true meaning of the 'independence' we were apparently granted 'on a platter of gold' (in the words of an early nationalist). Devolution of power is inevitable if we are to remain one country, as the leadership itself well knows, which is why they twice attempted to appease the clamour by convening pretend conferences. The first was in 2005 when President Olúṣẹ́gun Ọbásanjọ́ and the thirty-six state governors handpicked four hundred delegates to discuss our future, with the proviso that 'our disagreement must not lead to disintegration', after which Ọbásanjọ́ himself was to have the final say on which of the conference recommendations (if any) would be implemented.

Ṣóyínká, who was nominated without his consent, called it 'a distraction'. A similar charade was repeated in 2014 under Goodluck Jonathan, who made his name by being the only president to graciously concede defeat at the polls because 'my ambition is not worth the blood of any Nigerian'. He did it to enable the ascension to office of President Muhammadu Buhari, who had threatened to form an interim national government if he lost, which is ironic in the light of what was to happen in 2023, as detailed in this book's final chapter.

Meanwhile, let me make my own position quite clear. I don't believe that the break-up of the country is the way forward because I don't believe in yet more 'independent' but impoverished nations lorded over by elderly chiefs at the service of the 'colonial master', but I do believe we need to devolve power to the component parts – a big ask, I readily concede – as even the same colonial master understood. Sub-Saharan Africa, with fewer people than either China or India but with vastly more resources of every kind, must speak with one voice before it can get anywhere in the face of the global reality, but in saying this I have hardly said anything new: Nkrumah said it, Sankara said it, Fẹlá said it. Enough said.

1

Ṣòrọ̀ Sókè/Speak Up

Yesterday . . . a politician carried vigilante to where the pro-testers were, it turned into a brawl, one of them wanted to set gun na so boys rush gun commot from the nigga hand . . . Useless youth, instead of joining us in protest to salvage his future, he was busy doing maiguard [gateman/guard].
        – Witness to protests in Kogi State

On 8 October 2020, protests calling for an end to police brutality erupted in Nigeria. They were sparked by the murder of a young man by officers of the Special Anti-Robbery Squad (SARS) in front of a hotel in the town of Ughelli in Delta State five days earlier. A witness uploaded a video of the shooting on social media; it quickly went viral, whereupon the witness was himself arrested, further escalating matters. Two days later, another video surfaced showing the killing of a twenty-year-old, up-and-coming musician known as Sleek in Port Harcourt in neighbouring Rivers State the previous month.[1] Protestors soon took to the streets across a number of southern cities, including Lagos, Ìbàdàn and Ògbómọ̀ṣọ́, as well as Abuja in the Federal Capital Territory.

---

1 His real name was Daniel Chibuike Ikeaguchi. There is another musician also known as Sleek – real name Selick Idahosa – who currently lives in Canada, the choice destination of fleeing Nigerians over the last decade.

SARS itself was first launched in Lagos State in 1992 in response to a growing spate of armed robberies as the country reeled from rising inflation triggered by the devaluation of the naira, a consequence of the IMF-inspired structural adjustment programme under the military regime of the 'evil genius' General Ibrahim Babangida. Over time, SARS branches were established across the thirty-six states and Abuja, and they promptly won a reputation for overreach and violence. Their main targets were young men in flashy cars with smartphones and laptops, whom they accused of being 'Yahoo-Yahoo boys' – internet scammers – but SARS officers also 'randomly roam[ed] around the streets and pick[ed] up feminine-seeming boys, and even straight-passing men,' according to Matthew Blaise, an LGBTQ+ activist. 'They go through their phones, violating their privacy. When they see queer content, these people are beaten, extorted, assaulted, and even after this they are still outed to their loved ones.'[2]

Over time, the activities of SARS drew the attention of Amnesty International, which published a report in 2016, *You Have Signed Your Own Death Warrant*. The title was taken from the testimony of an unnamed thirty-three-year-old petrol station attendant in Awkuzu in Anambra State who was accused by his employer of organising a robbery at the premises the previous year:

> They brought a plain sheet and asked me to sign. When I signed it, they told me I have signed my death warrant. There were two policemen in the hall. They asked me if I knew how many people died there. They said that if I die, my blood will never be on their hands. They took me to the

---

2   Matthew Blaise, 'Queer Nigerians Are Being Beaten by SARS — I'm Trying to End That', *Out Magazine*, 13 October 2020.

back of the building and tied my hands to the back. They also connected the rope to my legs, leaving me hanging on a suspended iron rod. They put the iron rod in the middle between my hands and the leg with my head facing the ground. My body ceased to function. I went limp. The [investigating police officer] came at intervals and told me to speak the truth. I lost consciousness. When I was about to die they took me down and poured water on me to revive me.

I was tortured two more times. I was detained in cell 3, where there were about 30 people. I was not given any medical attention despite the fact that I was close to death. I was not allowed access to a lawyer, a doctor or my family.[3]

He was detained for two weeks and only released following a high court order. In the event, he was more fortunate than twenty-nine-year-old Emeka Egbo, who died in custody after he was arrested by SARS officers following a fight with a neighbour, as his brother discovered when he tried to visit him:

I gave the policeman at the gate the list of people I want to see. He said I must pay N1,000 (approx. US$4) each for every person I want to see. But I told him I do not have such kind of money. They refused to allow me see them. I came back the next day with two relatives, they ask us to pay N1,000 each. Again we could not afford to pay and were not allowed to see them. We were not told why they were arrested. We returned in the evening and were taken inside the SARS office after paying the money demanded by the policemen. The squad leader told me and five of our

---

3 Amnesty International, 'You Have Signed Your Own Death Warrant': Torture and other ill-treatment by Nigeria's special anti-robbery squads (SARS), 2016, 14–15.

relatives that Emeka is dead ... They said they were not responsible for the death of Emeka. We were not allowed to ask any questions or seek clarification.[4]

The family subsequently contacted a lawyer as well as the National Human Rights Commission. Both made repeated demands for an investigation, but nothing came of it, in this as in countless other such cases.

Criticism of SARS actually began soon after the country returned to democracy in 1999 following three decades of almost uninterrupted military rule, the end of which happened to coincide with the emergence of social media, which Nigerians took to with alacrity. In response to the growing public outrage, the government finally convened a committee in 2009 to look into abiding by the United Nations Convention against Torture, apparently oblivious of the fact that torture was not then proscribed in the criminal and penal codes. This was eventually rectified in 2017, the same year that the hashtag #EndSARS first appeared, whereupon the conveners were immediately branded 'criminals' by Jimọh Moshood, the police public relations officer, despite the fact that the inspector-general of police, Ibrahim Idris, had convened a three-day conference the previous year to address the problem. Typically, that was where the matter ended. According to Amnesty International, by 2020 there had been at least eighty-two cases of torture, ill-treatment and extrajudicial executions since its 2016 report, although we can be sure that the number is much higher given the unreliability of official statistics, in this as in all other areas of public life.[5]

---

4 Ibid., 16.

5 Amnesty International, *Time to End Impunity: Torture and other human rights violations by special anti-robbery squad (SARS)*, 2020, 9.

Again typically, no one has ever been charged, much less prosecuted.

It was against this background that Nigeria's youthful majority – more than 60 percent of the country's 220 million people are under twenty-four years of age – took to the streets. Under the #EndSARS banner, they presented the government with a five-point agenda: the immediate release of detained protestors; justice for deceased victims of police violence and appropriate compensation for their families; an independent body to oversee the investigation and prosecution of reported cases of police misconduct within ten days; the psychological evaluation and retraining of disbanded SARS operatives before being redeployed; and adequate pay for protecting lives and property.

This last was very much to the point. In common with the country's estimated 89,000 public servants, the police are provided with an office, a uniform and a stipend and tacitly encouraged to go and find their salaries from the public they purport to serve, which is why, according to Professor Adéwùnmí Adéṣínà, current president of the African Development Bank, Nigerians pay 'one of the highest implicit tax rates in the world'.[6] Simply put, it is impossible for an inspector, say, to live on ₦87,135 (US$209.545) a month – itself more than double the salary of a constable – in the absence of social safety nets, but unlike other government employees the police are unfortunate in being the visible, daily face of a venal system. Moreover, the casual resort to violence is part of their identity: like the army, their vocation is not to serve 'the people' but to subjugate 'the natives', hence their isolation in barracks, where they remain to this day.

---

6 'Nigerians pay one of world's highest "implicit tax rates" — Adesina', *Premium Times*, 21 January 2021.

The protests lasted a fortnight and were remarkable for their discipline in the face of a state which has only ever understood the language of violence, as the protestors themselves knew well enough. The first casualty, Isíákà Jimọh, was shot dead in Ògbómọ̀ṣọ́ in Ọ̀yọ́ State on Saturday, 14 October. That Sunday, protestors attacked the palace of the traditional king, Oba Jimọh Oyèwùmí, causing considerable damage. In the ensuing chaos, the police gunned down another three protestors: Ganíyù Moshood, Táíwò Adéọ̀yọ́ and Pẹ̀lúmi Ọlátúnjí. The state governor, Séyi Mákindé, sought to defuse the situation by giving each of the families of the deceased ₦1mn (US$2,400), but he betrayed the insensitivity of an entitled ruling class by offering the oba ₦100mn for the damage to his property. For his part, the 'father of all' graciously agreed to accept 'only' ₦10mn, having forgiven the 'hoodlums and miscreants' for 'their mistake and misdeed in the knowledge that they have retraced their steps and mended their ways for the future and will no longer allow themselves to be misguided'.[7]

A group known as the Feminist Coalition quickly took control of the movement. The brainchild of two women, Dámilọ́lá Òdúfúwà and Odúnayọ̀ Ewéniyi, it was launched in July 2020 to float a progressive group organised 'around the social, economic and political equality for Nigerian women in a more sustainable way'. Lacking prior experience, they were drawn to the #EndSARS protests because they believed that 'without structure, the protests could turn violent and women would be the most affected'. They proved remarkably adept at raising funds from Nigerians

---

7   Ola Ajayi, '₦100m gift: Soun of Ogbomoso rejects N90m', *Vanguard*, 21 October 2020.

both at home and abroad for hospital and legal bills to the tune of US$388,000, all accounted for in the interests of the transparency so lacking in the public sphere. They also set up Soro Soke Online Radio.

Clearly rattled, on 11 October President Buhari suddenly announced that the government was scrapping SARS 'with immediate effect'. He also promised to address the 'genuine concerns and agitations … about the excessive use of force and in some cases extrajudicial killings', and he assured the public that 'all those responsible for misconduct or wrongful acts' would be 'brought to justice', but this turned out to be a ruse. Just three days later, the government announced the formation of the Special Weapons and Tactics (SWAT) force to replace SARS, the American-inspired acronym betraying the lack of originality – not to say worship of all things foreign. Believing the matter now settled, the government upped the ante by having the army – not the police – issue a warning to 'all subversive elements and troublemakers' that it stood 'ready to fully support the civil authority in whatever capacity to maintain law and order and deal with any situation decisively'. Less than a week later, on 20 October, soldiers opened fire on peaceful demonstrators at the Lekki Toll Gate in Lagos.

'They just came with guns blazing,' recalled Obianuju Catherine Udeh, better known by the moniker DJ Switch, in a much-viewed CNN interview. A thirty-seven-year-old DJ and musician with a significant social media following, she had not been previously known for her political views, identifying instead as 'a tech junkie' who loved 'innovation and creativity', but she found herself drawn into the unfolding protests. As she said in another interview: 'I remember taking a picture on one of the days to say to my fans: if you have the opportunity to come out, do it, if you can't, just do it online, but whatever you do, you must speak up, because this affects all of us.'[8]

DJ Switch survived the shooting, which she live-streamed, gathering spent cartridges as she fled. In a subsequent post, she claimed that fifteen people were killed and that the soldiers carted away the corpses in order to hide the evidence. She also claimed that the soldiers were followed by former SARS officers in their familiar uniform, who continued the shootings. After a follow-up video she posted went viral, her manager received a phone call from a government official 'spitting fire and brimstone'. She subsequently fled the country in fear of her life and later turned up in Canada, where she addressed the parliament. At a press conference in Abuja the following month, Lai Mohammed, the information minister, denied that the security personnel had used live ammunition, called it 'a massacre without bodies' and dismissed DJ Switch as 'a fraud' and 'a front for divisive and destructive forces'. Confronted with the live-stream, he was forced to backtrack even as he sought to downplay the numbers.

Coincidentally, Bọ́lá Ahmed Tinúbú, the former two-term governor of Lagos State who would prevail in the February 2023 election, was himself accused of complicity with the authorities following an interview in which he appeared to blame the protestors themselves: 'Those who suffered casualties need to answer some questions too. Why were they there? How long were they there? What types of characters were they?' He then made matters worse by condemning the killings on the grounds that the

---

8 Suyin Haynes, 'She Livestreamed the Shooting of Peaceful Protesters in Lagos. Now in Exile, DJ Switch Is Still Fighting for the Future of Nigeria', *Time*, 17 December 2020.

soldiers should have used rubber bullets instead. It later turned out that the electronic billboard above the toll gate which had been switched off just before the soldiers arrived was owned by Tinúbú's son, Sèyi. There was even a rumour that Tinúbú had a stake in the US$40,000 that the toll gate rakes in daily and which the protestors had put at risk. Tinúbú himself denied the latter claim but it hardly mattered whether it was true or not. As we shall see, he has come to epitomise the tiny demographic of old men known as 'elders' who comprise less than 3.5 percent of the population aged over sixty-five but whose suffocating sense of entitlement – and our acquiescence in it – has been a convenient cover for the large-scale theft that has impoverished a country otherwise considered 'too rich to be poor'.

Following the massacre, the Feminist Coalition called off the protests on the grounds that 'no Nigerian life is worth losing to senseless violence'. By then, the great army of unemployed, under-employed and – in not a few cases – unemployable young men known as 'area boys', who had been encouraged to (unsuccessfully) provoke the protestors into violence, had already caused a great deal of damage, including the destruction of at least seventeen police stations which were wholly or partially razed in Lagos State. For reasons to be explored at greater length in the following chapter, the demonstrations were entirely confined to the south of the country. Indeed, there were a few seemingly spontaneous demonstrations in *favour* of SARS in Dutse, Kano and Maiduguri in the North; according to Ukkasha Hamza Rahuma, leader of the Northern Youth Assembly of Nigeria, it was imperative for everyone to 'join hands to support the reforming of SARS for optimum performance where no human right will be violated'. A political analyst, Máyọ̀wá Adébọ́lá, cited a disparity in police behaviour: 'Check the records for the brutality, for the murdering,' he

9

told the German broadcaster Deutsche Welle. 'It is all in the south, it does not get to the core north.'

However, a more sympathetic explanation for the divide was offered by a human rights lawyer, Audu Bulama Bukarti. According to him, SARS officers are just as 'vicious and corrupt' in the Northern Region but apply different techniques of coercion on the local Muslim population, who are on the whole less well-educated and more deferential. He also noted the deteriorating security situation since the return of democracy (or what passed as such) in 1999: 'They feel their biggest assailants are Boko Haram and the so-called bandits that kill and abduct dozens literally daily. Instead of dissipating time and energy protesting against SARS, which is a lesser evil, they reckon that it is better to use their resources on pressuring the government to tackle insecurity.'[9] Hashtags including #SecureNorthNow, #End-BokoHaramNow and #EndBanditryNow briefly trended.

For many – and I am one of them – the #EndSARS protests were a game-changer; in the words of Fakhrriyyah Hashim, also of the Feminist Collective: 'This is just the beginning of a youth awakening in Nigeria, of things that we can do to improve the state of the country. We will continue to do this, especially in the lives of women.' In fact, the central role of the Feminist Coalition in fighting for change is not unprecedented in what is an otherwise profoundly patriarchal society, hence the low representation of women at the public level. The 1929 Aba women's riots – also referred to as the 'Women's War' – were sparked by plans to tax traders in the South-east. Thousands of women joined protests that saw colonial shops and banks attacked and courts

---

9 Audu Bulama Bukarti, '#ENDSARS: There is no North-South divide', *African Arguments*, 17 October 2020.

burnt down, with the colonial administration finally admitting defeat. Eighteen years later, Fúnmiláyọ̀ Ransome-Kútì, mother of Fẹlá Kútì, successfully mobilised thousands of women in the South-west against a proposed tax on small traders. Dubbed the Lioness of Lisabi, she became an advocate for women's suffrage and a central figure in the fight for independence. Her Abẹòkúta Women's Union had an estimated 20,000 members known for their persistence; in the words of Ndi Kato, a gender activist who participated in #EndSARS: 'The history of Nigeria has had a lot of women come out to fight and push for their rights. Those battles strong women before us fought have been downplayed.'

But there is also the sense of a younger generation having come of age in a democracy (however flawed) but without any visible prospects: 'What have I benefited from this country since I was born?' one of the protesters asked, alluding to the worsening indicators at all levels and the country's high rate of unemployment, currently standing at over 33 percent and rising as the naira continues to plummet. According to the Manufacturing Association of Nigeria, 820 companies closed down between 2000 and 2008; since 2015, when the present administration assumed power, another 300 have gone the same way despite election promises to create three million jobs each year. And it continues to get worse. Not long ago, it was calculated that ₦1mn in November 2021 was worth just ₦350,000 exactly one year later.

By the time of the first anniversary of #EndSARS, there was despondency over the fact that nothing had changed, especially after some protestors gathered at that same Lekki Toll Gate and were tear-gassed for their trouble. At a parallel gathering in Abuja, Chioma Agwuegbo, a women's rights activist who was fired at with live rounds but survived, said that the security forces were initially 'a little careful' in the immediate wake of the shootings but have 'since returned to their bad behaviour', especially since no one has been held to account following the judicial panels of enquiry instituted across all thirty-six states. For one thing, seven northern states – Borno, Jigawa, Kano, Kebbi, Sokoto, Yobe and Zamfara – refused point-blank to comply. Those which did experienced long adjournments, with police officers refusing to show up when called upon to give testimony. In all, eighteen states concluded their hearings, but none have so far made their findings public, leading to accusations that they were just window-dressing, like so much else to do with government in Nigeria.

Others are more hopeful, for instance K. O. Bàbá Johnson, a Port Harcourt–based comedian who believes that while the movement 'might not have completely ended police brutality', it nevertheless brought it down substantially (as I have myself observed in Lagos): 'We've moved from the point where we'd wake up every day on social media and see police trying to march people in the gutter, flogging them with machetes, to now we only see these kinds of videos once or twice in a month.' In his opinion: 'I don't think anyone can successfully stop the average Nigerian who's dissatisfied, who's oppressed, from speaking up,' although he acknowledged some of the negative after-effects, for instance the ban on crypto-currencies used by the Feminist Coalition after their accounts were blocked by the central bank. And even the disillusioned Ms Agwuegbo agrees: 'I think the legacy of #EndSARS is that everyone has seen that the skills they use in their daily lives can be useful as far as taking back the country is concerned. Young people are organising for the 2023 elections. There's quite a bit of work being done.' Indeed so. All that energy was deployed in support of Peter Obi, the soft-spoken former two-term governor of Anambra State who spontaneously, and seemingly without warning, emerged as their presidential flag-bearer. Unlike Tinúbú and Atiku Abubakar, the former two-term vice president and the third of the leading triumvirate seeking the highest office, he didn't go around throwing bundles of cash to prove his credentials. For the first time in the country's history, the majority youths amassed behind a figure who promised them nothing but good governance in the hope of making the 'giant of Africa' worthy of the appellation instead of the poverty capital of the world that is our present lot.

2

In the Beginning; or, One-Chance[1]

Nothing could shake their conviction that if I put all their country down upon paper, and Mr Barter took pieces of all their trees and shrubs home, we should make charms of these things to use against them, and then return and take their country from them.

— Captain Glover

I wish to try whether we can succeed in ruling the country through the Fulani not by the Fulani ... Henceforth they must be our puppets and adopt our methods and rules.

— Frederick Lugard

There was nothing inevitable about the country that came to be called Nigeria, which began life in 1900 as two separate protectorates – Southern and Northern – along with the Crown Colony of Lagos before they were all amalgamated in 1914. According to George Goldie, its principal architect, the two entities were 'as widely separated in laws, government, customs, and general ideas about life, both in this world and the next, as England is from China'.[2] The South

---

1 'One-chance' is the name Nigerians use for a form of robbery that takes place in both public and private vehicles when people accept the offer of a ride.

2 Quoted in Max Siollun, *What Britain Did to Nigeria: A Short History of Conquest and Rule*, London: Hurst & Co, 2021, 320.

consisted of a plethora of ethnicities and languages which had co-existed for centuries without seeing any need to come together in a formal arrangement; it was also to become predominantly Christian and English-speaking following the activities of the European missionaries. The North, by contrast, was predominantly Islamic, spoke a common language in Hausa and had largely been ruled as a single entity following a jihad in 1804 by Fulani cattle-rearing nomads from the Sahel, who defeated the otherwise semi-autonomous emirates that had existed for centuries past. Indeed, the ill-conceived coupling of the protectorates was the only issue the early nationalists on either side agreed upon. In 1947, thirteen years before the country became independent, Ọbáfẹ́mi Awólọ́wọ̀, a southerner and the first leader of the opposition, called Nigeria 'a mere geographical expression', the very same year that Abubakar Tafawa Balewa, his northern counterpart and the first (and only) prime minister of Nigeria, said that 'it existed as one country only on paper'. The fact that the country actually achieved independence as a single entity is as miraculous as the fact that it continues to (just) cohere.

Matters were further complicated by the educational imbalance between the two regions. From the start, the ruling emirs of the Sokoto Caliphate, then Africa's largest pre-colonial state, were anxious to exclude missionaries and the schools that came with them on the grounds that access to foreign notions would ultimately undermine their authority. In this, they had the full support of the colonising power intent on ruling indirectly through them, much as the Fulani had themselves done; in the words of Sir (later Lord) Frederick Lugard, the man responsible for the amalgamation: 'In the great emirates of the north, we find the most advanced political organizations of tropical Africa, while in the hills, often only a short distance away from the Emir's capital, and in the southern forests, we find some of the most backward and atomic groups under our rule.'[3]

In the South, by contrast, with its diffuse centres of power, modern education was a means of upward social mobility. As a result, by the time of amalgamation over 97 percent of enrolled students were southerners, with the South hosting over 95 percent of all schools. This imbalance – which persists to this day – exercised the British from the start. As early as 1922, Sir Hugh Clifford, the then colonial administrator, noted that 'although the British had ruled in the north for more than 20 years they had not trained a single clerk, copyist or mechanic to serve in the administration, such personnel being recruited as desired from the south or from other colonies'.[4] He also pointed out that whatever education did exist 'has been allowed to become the almost exclusive prerequisite of the children of the ruling classes' – a phenomenon which still obtains. This ruling class thinks nothing of sending their own children to boarding schools and universities in the former colonial heartland while the *talakawa* – masses – are deprived of even primary education as part of the natural order of things. As a consequence, the North has the highest number of out-of-school children in the world, estimated by the UN at over 20 million as of October 2022.[5]

---

3   Margery Perham, 'Some Problems of Indirect Rule in Africa', *Journal of the Royal African Society*, Vol. 34, No. 135, April 1935, 7.

4   S. J. S. Cookey, 'Sir Hugh Clifford as Governor of Nigeria: An Evaluation', *African Affairs*, Vol. 79, No. 317, Oct. 1980, 6.

5   This is despite the ₦220bn credit facility from the World Bank under the Better Education Service Delivery for All in seventeen states of the federation in order to 'increase equitable access for out-of-school children, improve literacy and strengthen accountability at the basic education level'.

As if that wasn't enough, the North also lagged behind the South economically. Where the dense rain forests of the latter exported more palm oil – crucial to the industrial revolution – to Britain than the rest of West Africa combined, the former, at more than twice the land mass, was largely devoid of natural resources and increasingly arid the nearer one got to the Sahara. It was also landlocked. In other words, the North was unable pay its own way, hence the amalgamation; in the words of Lord Harcourt, the 'old roué' secretary of state for the colonies:

> We have released Northern Nigeria from the leading strings of the . . . Treasury. The promising and well-conducted youth is on an allowance 'on his own' and is about to effect an alliance with a Southern lady of means. I have issued the special licence and Sir Frederick will perform the ceremony . . . May the union be fruitful and the couple constant.[6]

Ironically, successive British governments were initially reluctant to annex what was to become a country more than three times the size of their own. The first problem was unfamiliar diseases, notably yellow fever and malaria, which took a heavy toll on Europeans: illness claimed a yearly average of 151 per 1,000 men between 1859 and 1875, giving West Africa its reputation as the 'White Man's Grave'.[7] There was also the terrain. The shallow creeks in the dense rain forests on either side of the newly mapped Niger River were difficult to navigate. British traders

---

6 Made in the course of a light-hearted after-dinner speech to the Colonial Service Club in 1913.

7 Philip D. Curtin, 'The End of the "White Man's Grave"? Nineteenth-Century Mortality in West Africa', *Journal of Interdisciplinary History*, Vol. 21, No. 1, Summer 1990, 70.

stationed on the coast relied on treaties signed between the Foreign Office (represented by a resident consul, also based on the coast) and the plethora of kings and chiefs nominally under British protection who delivered the precious palm oil to them, much as local potentates had once delivered the slaves the British outlawed when it became expedient.[8] But two events in 1884 proved decisive, by which time the use of quinine to treat malaria had become widespread. The first was the invention of the Maxim gun which changed the nature of warfare (much as the atomic bomb was to do in the following century):

> Where early nineteenth-century musket rifles took a whole minute to load, had a range of only 80 meters and misfired nearly a third of the time, this mass-murder device could expel 600 rounds of ammunition in a single minute, utilising energy from the recoil acting on the breech block to eject each spent cartridge and insert the next one, instead of a hand-operated mechanism.[9]

Local militias armed with Dane guns (flintlock muskets), pistols, machetes, spears, and bows and arrows were helpless against this 'devastating killing machine' that was

---

8 Some historians would disagree with this reading of events, for instance: 'This interpretation is in no small part influenced by the fact that British officials themselves promoted palm oil as a "legitimate" article of trade capable of replacing slaves ... This is simply not true. At the same time that the palm oil trade was increasing so rapidly, the slave trade continued to exist and even thrive in some places.' Toyin Falola and Matthew M. Heaton, *A History of Nigeria*, London: Cambridge University Press, 2008, 79–80.

9 Fola Fagbule and Feyi Fawehinmi, *Formation: The Making of Nigeria from Jihad to Amalgamation*, Cassava Republic: London & Abuja, 2020, 70.

quickly banned from sale in Africa. British forces could now act with impunity against recalcitrant rulers, most notoriously in the case of the oba of Benin, whose kingdom dated back to the thirteenth century and covered an area the size of Scotland – and also happened to control a great deal of the palm oil trade. Following what appears to have been a manufactured argument – a minor British official itching for a showdown claimed to have been snubbed by the oba, who at the time was observing a religious rite – a huge force was assembled to make him know that 'chief pass chief'.

The invading force was divided into three. A main column marched on the city while two 'flying' columns were deployed to the west and east in order to terrorise urban settlements. In all, about four million rounds of ammunition were discharged. No official death toll was recorded, although one English officer described 'quantities of dead natives killed during the fight' and another who said that the 'slaughter was enormous'. Local 'Houssa' soldiers who penetrated the bush said that they saw 'hundreds of dead bodies, some of which were simply cut in two by the Maxim fire'. The city was sacked and later destroyed, the oba exiled and the palace looted of its treasures, notably the so-called Benin bronzes which, having long adorned museums in Europe, the United States, Japan, Senegal and the UAE are currently the subject of restitution negotiations.

The second event of 1884 was the Berlin Conference, which was convened to put an end to the increasing clashes between the leading European powers – Belgium, Britain, France, Germany, Spain and Portugal – over African real estate. While it didn't settle all the outstanding claims, the conference managed to secure for Britain the region around the lower reaches of the Niger River, which became known as the Oil Rivers Protectorate. In theory, anyone was now free to conduct their business within this new possession, although the British moved quickly to establish a monopoly which, despite or because of the subterfuge, was the raison d'être of colonial rule.

The immediate casualty of this new order was a former indentured servant (although some say he was a slave) by the name of Mbanaso Okwara-Ozurumba but better known to history as King Jaja (or Ja Ja) of Opobo. Born around 1821, he rose to dominate the palm oil trade and at the height of his influence employed several thousand people. He also controlled a fleet of fifty canoes to patrol his domain but was by all accounts a self-effacing fellow, the better not to excite the envy of others. Describing himself as 'a poor, ignorant man' who didn't 'know book', he employed a freed African American woman from Kentucky by the name of Emma White to draft his correspondence as well as run the school he established. He nonetheless failed to fool Sir Richard Burton, the British consul, who described him as 'young, healthy and powerful and not less ambitious, energetic and decided', and added:

> He is the most influential man and the greatest trader in the river and £50,000, it is said, may annually pass through his hands. He lives much with Europeans and he rides rough-shod over young hands coming into Bonny. In a short time he will either be shot or he will beat down all his rivals.[10]

The Foreign Office concurred: 'Jaja is the ablest of the coast middlemen. He is a man of energy and considerable ability . . . he is sharp enough to hold his own with the

---

10   Ibid., 148.

Europeans and powerful enough to overcome the natives in the interior.'[11]

As might be expected of such an astute operator, he carefully studied the new treaty he was expected to sign and which, for the first time, granted British merchants the exclusive right to trade in his domain under the protection of the queen. He asked the British consul, Edward Hyde Hewett, what was meant by 'protection'. He also asked for written assurance that it would not in any way affect his own authority, which he duly received:

> I write, as you request, with reference to the word 'protection' as used in the proposed Treaty, that the Queen does not want to take your country or your markets, but at the same time is anxious no other natives should take them. She undertakes to extend her gracious favour and protection, which will leave your country still under your government. She has no wish to disturb your rule.[12]

However, the following year, in accordance with the General Act of the Berlin Conference which provided for freedom of navigation on the Niger River and its tributaries (and which, needless to say, neither Jaja nor any other African chief was party to), the Foreign Office declared a protectorate over the area otherwise covered by the treaty Jaja had signed but which Hewett now abrogated.

By and by, Hewett returned to Britain and was replaced by Harry Johnston, a 'headstrong, imperialistically minded young careerist', who took an instant dislike to Jaja.[13] Calling him 'the most grasping, unscrupulous and overbearing

---

11 Siollun, *What Britain Did to Nigeria*, 54.
12 Ibid., 55.
13 Ibid.

of mushroom Kings who ever attempted to throttle the growing commerce of white men with the rich interior', Johnston
complained that 'here is the country where white men may
hope to settle and enjoy good health, and it is from lands
like these that runaway slaves and upstart Kings like Ja Ja
are trying to keep us from penetrating'. He then demanded
that Jaja sign an amendment to his treaty allowing free trade
or face a naval expedition. Jaja refused and insisted instead
that he would prefer to deal with his 'father', that is, Hewett,
when he returned but Johnston was adamant. Still not done,
Johnston invited him to a meeting on board a ship. Jaja at
first refused, saying that he was 'quite sensible' of Johnston's
'position' and his 'capability' of harming him but relented
when the latter swore on his sacred 'word' as a true-born
Englishman that no harm would befall him:

> I have summoned you to attend in a friendly spirit. I hereby
> assure you that whether you accept or reject my proposal
> tomorrow no restraint whatever will be put upon you, you
> will be free to go as soon as you have heard the message of
> the government. If you do not attend the meeting no further
> consideration will be shown you, and you will be simply
> treated as an enemy of the British government. I shall
> proclaim your deposition, and hand your markets over to
> the Bonny men. If you attend tomorrow I pledge you my
> word that you will be free to come and go.[14]

But no sooner did Jaja board than Johnston made him an
offer he couldn't refuse:

> Should you be so misguided as to refuse to submit to the
> orders of the British Government it will be taken as an

---

14   Ibid., 61.

admission that you are guilty of the charges brought against you. I shall then proceed to use an armed force, which will mercilessly crush any resistance you may offer. You will be deposed, and tried for your misdeeds, as a common malefactor; your property will be confiscated, and your country brought to ruin by the stoppage of trade. Should you attempt to evade me by escaping into the interior you will be declared an outlaw, a reward will be offered for your capture, which will be sufficiently large to tempt the greed of your treacherous followers, and your bitter enemies among the surrounding tribes . . . will be free to avenge on you old grievances. No man ever stood in a more critical position than you are in at the present moment, King Ja Ja . . . But refuse to do so, and you leave this Court a ruined man for ever, cut off from your people and your children.[15]

Jaja surrendered and was immediately transported to the Gold Coast (present-day Ghana), where he was charged with violating the terms of his treaty. In a reversal of British legal doctrine, he was obliged to prove himself innocent. But a show trial is a show trial. Jaja was found guilty of two of the three charges and exiled to the Caribbean island of St Vincent. Lord Salisbury, the British prime minister, initially professed himself unhappy with the kidnapping – 'To invite a chief on board your ship, carefully concealing the fact that you have any designs against his person, and then, when he has put himself in your power, to carry him away, is hardly legitimate warfare, even if we had a right to go to war' – but then retroactively enacted the Opobo Political Prisoners Detention Ordinance that allowed Jaja to be investigated.[16] In exile and with only one of his wives,

---

15   Ibid., 62.
16   Ibid., 58.

Patience, who was allowed to accompany him, Jaja underwent a rapid deterioration of his health. After four years and much pleading, he was finally allowed to return home, but only after he had signed an undertaking to remain a private citizen, abstain from fomenting disturbances and conduct himself with loyalty to the Crown. Unfortunately, he died on the way back, ostensibly from drinking poisoned tea, and was buried in Opobo amid much fanfare. In 1903, a bronze statue of him was commissioned and has since been elevated to a national monument.

The way was now left open for George Goldie to take over. Born in 1846 into an aristocratic Scottish-Manx family which had made some of its fortune from the African slave trade, he was described by a contemporary as a 'fair, thin, young man with piercing blue eyes looking [like] something between a vulture and a mummy'.[17] He qualified as an engineer from the Royal Military Academy in Woolwich but unexpectedly inherited a fortune before he could decide on a career and vowed henceforth to 'lead a life of dissipation'. However, an opportunity to become a more productive citizen presented itself when a family member asked him to invest in a company which traded along the Niger River and its tributary, the Benue River. In 1877, he embarked on a tour and quickly 'conceived the ambition of adding the region . . . to the British Empire', and this at a time when British interest in acquiring new territories was at its nadir: just a few years earlier, a House of Commons Select Committee had advised against 'all further acquisitions of territory or assumption of government, or new treaties offering any protection to native tribes' with the exception of Sierra Leone, which was being used as a naval base and refuge for intended slaves freed by British

---

17   Fagbule and Fawehinmi, *Formation*, 165.

squadrons patrolling the West African coast. Goldie nevertheless incorporated what was to become the Royal Niger Company (RNC), which immediately set about buying up the competition. After years of lobbying, he was finally granted a royal charter in 1886, which effectively turned the company into a government with the power to levy taxes, establish an armed constabulary and sign (one-sided) treaties with local rulers even as King Jaja was about to be transported to a faraway Caribbean island, much as Goldie's forebears had done with the 203 Angolan slaves they had shipped off to Barbados.

As one might expect, the treaties themselves – anywhere between 250 and 500 – were exclusive, perpetual and failed to state whether they were covered by English or native law. A neurotically secretive man, Goldie once told a friend that 'the less you say about me the happier I shall be,' and he swore his children to silence and took care to destroy his company's records when he was finally forced out in 1900. What is known is that he was 'violent and uncompromising' with 'a good deal of uncontrolled temper'. His company's constabulary, which consisted of between 400 and 500 men commanded by officers loaned by the British army and equipped with the dreaded Maxim gun, undertook at least 56 operations, mostly in the South-east, and sometimes even outside the RNC's 'jurisdiction' – against communities which attempted to resist his designs.

Such, for instance, was the fate of the people of Nembe, fisherfolk for the most part, who resided in the watery landscape of the Niger Delta, a people who were to enhance by an astronomical percentage the dowry brought to the promising northern youth by the southern lady of means when crude oil was discovered in commercial quantities in 1956. Suddenly, the Nembe were required to procure an array of prohibitively expensive licenses in order to trade with neighbouring communities within RNC territory because, as Goldie claimed, they were 'a class of men . . . who were formerly the worst enemies of civilisation in central Africa. These were disreputable coloured men who . . . lived by surreptitious dealings and slaves . . . stirring up the natives to discontent and bloodshed.' Faced with starvation, they finally rose up in revolt and attacked the company's main factory at Akassa in the early hours of 29 January 1895. They destroyed most of the property, sank two ships, killed twenty-four labourers and took sixty hostages, most of whom they later executed. The reprisal was swift. Less than a month later, the Foreign Office despatched four ships with 150 sailors and marines to back the RNC's own constabulary. Several Nembe towns and villages were torched and several hundred inhabitants killed.

Yet this incident was to prove a watershed. A commission of inquiry a few months later noted the heavy involvement of government forces, which couldn't take orders from a private company, and recommended that RNC territory should come under the direct control of the Crown. This also happened to chime with the new thinking in London. That same year, the new secretary of state for the colonies, Joseph Chamberlain, recently described as 'alternatively demagogue, Nonconformist, atheist, republican, imperialist, capitalist, statist and "socialist" of sorts',[18] gave a speech in which he declared the British 'the greatest of the governing races that the world has ever seen', and opined that it was pointless occupying such vast spaces 'unless you can make the best of them'.[19] Five years later, the RNC's charter was revoked and the company wound down. On 1

---

18   Owen Hatherley, 'No Mythology, No Ghosts', *London Review of Books*, Vol. 44, No. 21, 3 November 2022.

19   Fagbule and Fawehinmi, *Formation*, 187.

January 1900, Britain formally declared the protectorates of Southern and Northern Nigeria, having decided that the vast, unprofitable area above the Niger River was also to be incorporated into the imperial design.

The main impetus for the conquest of the North seems to have been rivalry with France, which was intent on colonising as much of West Africa as possible and largely succeeded in doing so. As in the South, it was Goldie who led the way in 1894 when he invited Frederick Lugard, a soldier who had distinguished himself in East Africa, to lead an RNC detachment to the town of Nikki in the upper Niger in order to sign a treaty with the king before the French could do so. He appeared at first to have succeeded, arriving just ahead of his imperial rival, but eventually lost out on a technicality – he signed with the wrong person – before he was called upon to lead the newly established West African Frontier Force to confront the Sokoto Caliphate, which the French, occupied elsewhere, conceded to the British before a shot was even fired.

Lugard himself made a great fuss about ending the slavery that had once again become endemic in the region – up to half the estimated population of ten million – as a result of the conquering Fulanis' policy of indirect rule. In fact, this was just an excuse. Neither Lugard in particular, nor the British government in general cared one way or the other, as indeed the southerners knew all too well with the so-called 'forced labour' that was used to build railways, roads and telegraphs, as well as carry white people about in hammocks. Those who were conscripted for a project had to work far from home without pay while also providing their own food, which only added insult to injury. They were also harshly treated because, according to Walter Egerton, governor of the Southern Protectorate from 1904 to 1912, any 'undue leniency' was 'apt to be construed by the natives and regarded as weakness'. Worse yet, the 'natives' could even be compelled to work against their personal interests, for instance clearing their own land to make way for a road or a railway without compensation, and this for the exclusive convenience of European trade. The British themselves were well aware of what they were doing; as one army officer observed: 'The problem of getting labour – which must be forced – and food supplies is manifestly difficult ... Moreover, no native likes working far away for an unknown white man under new conditions, on a job he does not understand,' although in 1906 Winston Churchill, then under-secretary of state for the Colonial Office, defended the practice in Parliament: 'In West African Colonies and Protectorates in which there is legal power to demand labour on roads and waterways, the Governor or High Commissioner alone can make an order that such work shall be done.'[20]

In the North specifically, there is some dispute over whether the so-called farm slavery that obtained there was the same as chattel slavery in, say, the United States, Brazil and Haiti, given that slaves in the Protectorate had certain rights, for instance the right to purchase their freedom (recognised as such under Muslim law), and to work on their own account when they were not required to work on their master's farm. Whatever the case, Lugard's edict outlawing the institution was only meant to absolve the new overlords from paying compensation to slave owners for freed slaves, as the British had done when they abolished the Atlantic trade they had previously profited so

---

20 Great Britain Parliament, *Hansard's Parliamentary Debates*, Arkose Press: San Mateo, CA, 2015, 119.

handsomely from over three centuries.[21] As Lugard himself later acknowledged, the object was 'gradually' to eradicate the institution while 'avoiding such hasty and ill-considered action as would dislocate the whole social framework in Muslim states, and result in pauperising and destroying the ruling classes which it was the object of Government to preserve and strengthen'.[22] And in his 1919 *Political Memoranda* he actually wrote in support of slavery as it applied to areas under Muslim jurisdiction:

> Generally speaking, the intention and policy of Government is not to interfere with the relation of master and slave, in the Northern Provinces, so long as the relation is voluntarily maintained by both parties, in districts which recognise Moslem law and are under the jurisdiction of Moslem Courts, but to abolish the status of slavery, absolutely and entirely, throughout every other district in Nigeria.[23]

Purporting to abolish slavery, which in fact persisted for another two generations, was also a useful cover to unseat the 'sensuous, avaricious and cruel' emirs who opposed Lugard and replace them with more pliable ones. The first

---

21 In 1833, Britain used 40 percent of its national budget, or about 5 percent of its GDP, to compensate the 3,000 slave-owning families for the loss of their 'property'. The property, in turn, not only got nothing but were made to work as 'apprentices' – for free – for another four years. Such a large sum of money – £20mn then, £2bn today – wasn't paid off until 2015, meaning that it was British taxpayers who footed the bill. The family of David Cameron, the former British prime minister, was among those compensated.

22 Polly Hill, 'From Slavery to Freedom: The Case of Farm-Slavery in Nigerian Hausaland', *Comparative Studies in Society and History*, July 1976, Vol. 18, No. 3, 407.

23 Ibid., 410.

to go was the emir of Bida, who had been deposed by Goldie four years earlier but had reclaimed his throne when RNC troops pulled out. Next was the emir of Kontagora, otherwise known as 'The Destroyer', who, upon hearing of Lugard's edict, vowed to die 'with a slave in my mouth'. Lugard then took a short break to return home, where he fell in love with Flora Shaw, Goldie's former lover and the person widely (but wrongly) believed to have coined the country's name. They later married. Returning in early 1903, he descended on Kano, which lay undefended because the emir had travelled to Sokoto to pay homage to the new sultan, who became Lugard's next target. He then marched on Katsina, which offered no resistance, followed by Zaria, and then, finally, Burmi in the far North-east. He would later claim that 'the British conquest of this vast country has been almost bloodless', although how he arrived at this conclusion is a mystery: in the second battle of Burmi, for instance, 'the WAFF fired an astonishing 32,710 rounds from small arms and piles of 700–1000 native corpses littered the town', among them the emir and two of his sons. The WAFF lost just thirteen.

With the fall of Burmi, Lugard was now king of the North. His domain would grow when the two protectorates were merged, eventually making Nigeria the only country in the world evenly split between Christians and Muslims. Unfortunately for the South, Lugard also ensured that the North (and, specifically, the minority Fulani who made up between a quarter and a third of the population) retained its ascendancy under British rule.[24] To this end, the British

---

24 To give one example: under the administration of Admiral Mustafa Nyako in Adamawa State (2007 to 2011), when we were supposedly enjoying the 'dividends of democracy' (an overused term I am in danger of overusing myself), ten of the fourteen commissioners

packed the army with northerners, having identified them as a 'martial race' as far back as the 1860s. Nor did they disappoint when called upon to put down 'revolts' in the South. Amalgamation only sped up the process, so much so that Hausa was made the army's language of command, with British officers required to take courses and exams in it in order to earn promotion.

In retrospect, one of the remarkable things about the formal colonisation of Nigeria was just how briefly it lasted. The British were initially confident of ruling for ninety-nine years, which was why Joyce Cary, the novelist who spent time in the country as a civil servant, could confidently write in *The Case for African Freedom* (1941) about the Africans' inability to rule themselves – 'You cannot give liberty to people by a wave of the hand, as you throw open a cage. If you attempted it you would find that your poor victims, like caged birds forced loose, would only injure or poison themselves' – even as Harold Macmillan's 'winds of change' were about to start blowing. Chinua Achebe was to write *Things Fall Apart* in direct response to Cary's attempt to depict a native in his otherwise celebrated *Mr Johnson*.[25] As it happens, the British were forced to

---

and the heads of all the institutions of higher learning were Fulani, yet they comprised just 3 percent of the population.

25 'At the university I read some appalling European novels about Africa (like Joyce Cary's much praised *Mister Johnson*) and realized that our story could not be told for us by anyone else no matter how gifted or well-intentioned.' Chinua Achebe, *Hopes and Impediments: Selected Essays, 1965–1987*, 1988: London: Heinemann, 38. All his classmates expressed disgust at the 'bumbling idiot of a character whom Joyce Cary and [their] teacher were so assiduously passing off as a poet when he was nothing but an embarrassing nitwit'. Chinua Achebe, *Home and Exile*, Oxford: Oxford University Press, 23. On the other

concede to nationalist pressure in the wake of the Second World War and bow out in 1960. On the one hand, Britain, along with the other colonial powers, emerged diminished even as the new superpowers – the United States and the Soviet Union – were hostile to the colonial project for reasons of their own; on the other, Nigerians themselves, like subject people elsewhere, had woken up to their diminished status in a world which had otherwise fought for freedom. This was especially true of those who had travelled abroad, some to study, others to fight, all to be changed by the experience. Prior to that, the relatively small number of educated, largely Lagos-based Nigerians, who were generally despised by colonial officers – Lugard: 'His loud and arrogant conceit are distasteful to me, his lack of natural dignity and courtesy antagonize me' – were more or less content to accept their place in the scheme of things.[26] Known collectively as Saros, some were returnees from Brazil and Cuba especially and others were freed would-be slaves from Sierra Leone. To one modern commentator, they were 'deluded hybrids' and 'a cowardly set of irresponsible deserters of the unlettered chiefs and masses' who 'smoothed the path of the foreign adventurer' for their own personal gain; but while this was undoubtedly true of most (both then and now), it could hardly be said to have applied to Herbert Macaulay, the man generally regarded as the father of Nigerian nationalism.[27]

---

hand, he thought Conrad's *Heart of Darkness* 'racist', but let us not get diverted.

26 Margery Perham, *Lugard: The Years of Authority, 1898–1945*, London: Collins, 1960, 506.

27 E. A. Ayandele, *Educated Elite in the Nigerian Society*, London University Press, 1974; quoted in P. Olisanwuche Esedebe, 'The Educated Elite in Nigeria Reconsidered', *Journal of the Historical Society of Nigeria*, Vol. 10, No. 3, December 1980, 113.

Born in Lagos in 1864, he was related on his mother's side to Samuel Àjàyí Crowther, returnee from Sierra Leone who rose to become the first African bishop of the Church of England. After leaving school at sixteen, Macaulay was appointed a clerical assistant and indexer of Crown land grants in the Public Works Department. Within three years, he was promoted to draughtsman and clerk and then awarded a scholarship to the UK, where he studied civil engineering and surveying, becoming the first Nigerian to qualify in both. He returned home in 1894 and was appointed a surveyor of Crown lands but lasted only five years because he was unhappy that his pay was less than half that of his British counterparts, although by then he had established himself as a player who 'electrified social life in Lagos', a 'regular feature at the various "at homes", "conversaziones", concerts, shows etc that were part of the Lagos society'. It was in these settings that 'he came to acknowledge the gift that was to stand him in good stead during his quarrel with the government', which was 'his remarkable genius for organising things and people'.[28]

Macaulay set up in private practice but finances were tight because few Nigerians could afford his services and the colonial authorities ensured that he never got any government contracts; it also didn't help that the same authorities accused him of corrupt practices during his tenure, specifically that he used his position 'to help friends acquire crown grants and persecute enemies by granting their lands to others', and also of 'buying crown lands under false names and selling them at a profit'. However, his real problem came in 1913 when he was accused of misappropriating £350 (£47,000 today) from the estate of one Mary

---

28 Patrick Cole, *Modern and Traditional Elites in the Politics of Lagos*, London: Cambridge University Press, 1975, 111.

Franklin, a freed slave who had made him the executor of her will. Macaulay claimed that he used the money to pay off debts owed by the estate but he was found guilty and sentenced to two years in prison, automatically barring him from holding elective office under the 1923 Clifford Constitution which, for the first time, allowed for four elected representatives to sit on the Lagos Legislative Council.

Not to be silenced, Macaulay became a regular contributor to the *Nigerian Chronicle*, a weekly newspaper established in 1908. In 1927, he and a friend, John Akinladé Caulcrick, a physician and politician, bought out the *Lagos Daily News*, the first daily newspaper in West Africa (motto: 'The safety of the people is the greatest law'). His journalism led to his second stint in prison following an article which claimed that a car bringing back a deposed oba from exile (in large part thanks to Macaulay himself, who had argued his case before the Privy Council in London) would be blown up by the oba's opponents. To the authorities, this was a rumour intended to fuel existing tensions within the colony and he was sentenced to six months. But the paper's main purpose was to trumpet the cause of the Nigerian National Democratic Party (NNDP), the country's first political party, which Macaulay had founded in response to the new constitution. The party's candidates won all seats in the 1923, 1928 and 1933 elections, but their presence was largely symbolic since they had no real powers, which were otherwise vested in the British-dominated Executive Council. Indeed, the NNDP was widely criticised on those grounds but there is no evidence that Macaulay (or any of the other 'deluded hybrids') was interested in radically confronting colonial rule at any deeper level – 'One feels that the elected leadership of the NNDP was less hostile to colonialism than most of the indigenous population, who believed that Macaulay would be able to free them from colonial rule'[29] – and this perception is borne out in the preamble to the NNDP's constitution, which pledged 'to maintain an attitude of unswerving loyalty to the throne and person of His Majesty the King Emperor, by being strictly constitutional in the adoption of its methods and general procedure.'[30]

But this is hardly surprising given the rigs of the times. Indeed, most would have subscribed to the views of Macaulay's former friend turned arch enemy, Henry Carr, a lifelong civil servant of apparently considerable ability for whom Macaulay was 'an evil genius' leading 'a little clique of ambitious and vainglorious men' intent on political power.[31] A devout Christian, Carr was assuredly one of the 'deluded hybrids' in his loud contempt for his backward brethren who lived a life of 'apprehension and alarm, of dread and terror [with] little or no reflection on life and its meaning [and no] sense of morality'.[32] That being so they needed 'severe discipline' to keep them in line.[33] In the context of the time, this meant flogging natives naked – men and women alike – in the marketplace, as the *Lagos Daily News* never tired of lamenting.

Macaulay's dominance of Lagos politics came to an end with the emergence of the more radical Nigerian Youth Movement in 1936. Although equally Lagos-based, its avowed aim was to create a truly pan-Nigerian party that would unite the plethora of ethnicities throughout the country. Within just two years, it had established forty

---

29   Ibid., 122.
30   Quoted in James S. Coleman, *Nigeria: Background to Nationalism*, Berkley: University of California Press 1960, 198.
31   Ibid., 113.
32   Ibid., 107.
33   Ibid., 106.

branches in the main urban areas outside Lagos and boasted a membership of 20,000 as it called for greater Nigerian participation in the civil service and government, along with universal suffrage for all citizens over the age of twenty-one (and not just Lagos-based males with landed property). To that end, it also wanted an end to the system of indirect rule fondly theorised by Goldie:

> Even an imperfect and tyrannical native African adminis-
> tration, if its extreme excesses were controlled by European
> supervision, would be, in the early stages, productive of far
> less discomfort to its subjects than well-intentioned but
> ill-directed efforts of European magistrates, often young
> and headstrong, and not invariably gifted with sympathy
> and introspective powers. If the welfare of the native races
> is to be considered, if dangerous revolts are to be obviated,
> the general policy of ruling on African principles through
> native rulers must be followed for the present.[34]

As became apparent, this was dubious logic but it also had the advantage of minimising the number of British personnel who would otherwise have been needed; and although it worked well enough in the North, where it was merely a continuation of what had already existed for a century under the Fulani, it was a different matter in the South, even in those parts where kings and chiefs existed in the first place. This was especially true among the Yorùbá in the South-west, which also happened to contain the highest concentration of educated people, who were excluded from local government even as they had to bend the knee to petty, often illiterate tyrants, but the system was even more resented in parts of the South-east where the institution of

---

34 Siollun, *What Britain Did to Nigeria*, 296.

royalty was unknown. In this case, the British simply appointed whomever they deemed worthy, for instance anyone happy to act as an informant against their own people, which caused them to be despised all the more, as noted in a discussion of the practice in 1934 by the African Society and the Royal Society of the Arts:

> Indirect rule was making puppets of African chiefs . . . they were chiefs in name only. If the chiefs were called agents it would be a better name because they were carrying out the orders of the British Government. The chiefs represented the people no longer, and the Africans did not want their chiefs to sell the people to the British. That was what indirect rule was doing.[35]

And yet, because the chiefs had great powers, indirect rule quickly came to be seen as a lucrative sideline. These powers included forcibly conscripting people to work on colonial projects, adjudicating legal cases and collecting taxes, the last of which was especially resented.

As it turned out, the Nigerian Youth Movement, which replaced Macaulay's party in the 1938 Lagos elections, was soon riven by internal conflict. Ironically, this was the result of its very diversity, as revealed when one of its rising stars, Benjamin Nnamdi Azikiwe, an Igbo from the South-east, accused some of the leading Yorùbá leaders among them of ethnic bias. In 1944, he left to form the National Council of Nigeria and the Cameroons (NCNC), which became the first political party to call explicitly for an end to colonial rule. 'Zik of Africa', as he soon became known, had returned home in 1937 after a long sojourn in the United States, where he acquired several degrees and associated

---

35 Ibid., 288–9.

with some of the leading African American intellectuals and activists, including W. E. B. Du Bois, Langston Hughes and Countee Cullen, and a short stint in the Gold Coast (present-day Ghana), where he fired up Kwame Nkrumah, that country's future president.[36] Described as 'fiery, tempestuous, young and extremely radical', Azikiwe effectively took over Macaulay's mantle even as he reached out to the now elderly firebrand and made him the party's first chairperson, with himself as secretary-general. Macaulay died two years later at the age of eighty-one, leaving Azikiwe to lead the party to the country's independence. Azikiwe also launched his own daily newspaper, the *West African Pilot* (motto: 'Show the light and the people will find the way').

Unfortunately for Azikiwe, his ambition for the NCNC to be a pan-Nigerian party fell victim to the 'Nigerian factor'. As pointed out in the preface to this book, although the country has over 250 ethnic groups, just three of them – the Hausa-Fulani in the North, the Igbo in the South-east and the Yorùbá in the South-west – made up fully two-thirds of the then population of 32 million, a state of affairs recognised for administrative purposes in 1939, when the British accordingly divided the country into three regions. All three, then as now, are mistrustful of each other but between them maintain what has been called a 'balance of terror', whereby any two will team up against the third to keep it in

---

36 In his autobiography, Nkrumah had this to say: 'My nationalism was also revived . . . through articles written in *The African Morning Post* by Nnamdi Azikiwe, a Nigerian from Onitsha. Azikiwe was himself a graduate from an American university and when I had first met him after he had addressed a meeting of the Gold Coast Teachers' Association some years earlier in Accra, I had been greatly impressed by him and had been more determined than ever to go to America.' Nkrumah, *Ghana: The Autobiography of Kwame Nkrumah*, Edinburgh: Thomas Nelson and Sons, 1957, 22.

check, with the minorities left to shift as best they might, with sometimes tragic results (as we shall see in the next chapter). Sure enough, two other parties filled in the ethnic gaps: the Northern People's Congress (NPC) and the Action Group (AG). The first, as its name implies, emerged in 1949 with the sole purpose of representing the interests of the Hausa-Fulani, hence its slogan: One North, One People. As its leader, Ahmadu Bello, openly stated, it was not for him 'to liquidate his grandfather's empire'.[37] The AG, founded in 1951, represented the people of the South-west and, as with Azikiwe's NCNC, was avowedly nationalist in outlook. All three parties took advantage of the 1946 Richards Constitution which, attempting to satisfy growing calls for representation, vouchsafed a House of Assembly to each of the regions, along with a federal House of Representatives where all could meet to discuss matters of common concern. Nobody was satisfied, albeit for different reasons. The

---

37 It should be said that this was not the first political party to emerge in the North. The little-known (and short-lived) Northern Elements Progressive Union was founded in 1945 by one Alhaji Raji Abdallah, whose view of the colonial adventure was uncompromising: 'Our rights as human beings were taken away by the Royal Niger Company on the 1st of June 1885 at Wurno. Our elders knew not then. But today we know. Shall we like cowards who die many times before their deaths fail to fight for the restoration of these rights? Is it life that is so dear or peace so sweet? No comrades, I for one pray to Allah to give me liberty or let me die.' Membership was 'open to all sons and daughters of Northern Nigeria, literate or illiterate, irrespective of language, locality or creed'. Many of its members were either civil servants or employees of the Native Administration, which made them vulnerable to both the established local and foreign authorities; Abdallah himself was sacked as a senior wireless and monitor operator in the Posts and Telegraph Department in 1947; see G. O. Olúsanya, 'Political Awakening in the North: A Re-Interpretation', *Journal of the Historical Society of Nigeria*, December 1967, Vol. 4, No. 1, 126, 127.

South was unhappy that the regional and national houses exercised no real powers, which continued to reside in the British-dominated Nigerian Legislative Council; the North was unhappy that it was allocated less than half the seats in the national legislature, given that it represented half the country's population, and it threatened to 'ask for separation from the rest of Nigeria on the arrangements existing before 1914' if this wasn't reversed.[38]

At bottom was the northern fear of southern domination once the British departed. There was, as we have seen, the educational imbalance whereby only 2 percent of the people in the Northern Region were literate in Roman script (and only 1 percent in the exclusively Muslim areas of the far north) compared with 16 percent in the Eastern Region and 18 percent in the Western Region. Additionally, there was just a single university graduate in the whole of the North as compared to hundreds in the South. This meant that the North couldn't even begin to staff its own civil service when the British left and would rely instead on southerners. This idea was so abhorrent that in a 1960 BBC interview Ahmadu Bello threatened to hire foreigners – including the British – ahead of other Nigerians to make up the numbers. This was the same interview in which he famously showed his disdain for the Igbo, 'whose desire is mainly to dominate everybody' wherever they happen to find themselves, although he was far from alone in this assessment, which was shared especially by the minorities in the Niger Delta.

The other problem was economic, hence the amalgamation in the first place, now exacerbated by the outpost of

---

38 Quoted in Tekena N. Tamuno, 'Separatist Agitations in Nigeria since 1914', *Journal of Modern African Studies*, Vol. 8, No. 4, December 1970, 567.

progress the South had become in the decades since. Railway links were built from the North to Lagos in 1912 and Port Harcourt in 1926 which dramatically increased the value of the North's exports from about £180,000 in 1910 to about £65,000,000 in 1962 (instead of £963,636 it would have been in real terms if it had remained the same). While a return to the pre-colonial trans-Saharan route 'may have been a romantic dream held by some Northern secessionists', the reality was that 'the North [was] utterly dependent on the Southern ports for its economic ties to the outside world' and would not have 'willingly let complete control of these ports, and the rail links to them, fall into entirely separate and potentially hostile hands' whatever their private reservations.[39]

The North threatened secession again two years later, on 1 April 1956, when the AG's Anthony Enahoro unexpectedly sponsored a motion calling for independence. This embarrassed the colonial administration, which hadn't expected such a development, and the motion was only defeated by the northern bloc's control of half the seats, and the motion was altered to read 'as soon as practicable'. The North wanted to secede but knew that was economically impractical so were happy for the British to remain in place while they dithered over how to solve an intractable problem. For their stand, the northern delegates alleged that they suffered abuse from Lagos mobs, which in turn led to rioting between northerners and southerners in Kano following the arrival in that city of an AG delegation on a political tour. In an emergency session, the Northern House of Assembly, together with the Northern House of Chiefs, endorsed an eight-point programme which, among other

---

39 Charles R. Nixon, 'Self-Determination: The Nigeria/Biafra Case', *World Politics*, July 1972, Vol. 24, No. 4, 489.

things, provided for virtually independent regional governments. Under this programme, there was to be a non-partisan executive central agency responsible for common services, including defence, external affairs, customs and West African research institutions. According to Bello, this represented 'our compromise on the suggestion of secession from Nigeria, as it then was'.

In response, British Secretary of State for the Colonies Oliver Lyttelton invited delegates to London to discuss a revision of the existing constitution. During the conference, which took place between July and August 1953, the delegates agreed on a federation of autonomous regions. The AG delegation also demanded the recognition of the 'right' of secession on the grounds that the 'dream' of a united Nigeria would otherwise fail, that is, that federalism could only work if it was based on the consent of the people. In the light of what was to happen within the first decade of independence, it was ironic that Azikiwe should have opposed Awólọ́wọ̀'s demand on the grounds that constitutions rarely provided for their own termination; he ultimately got his way in the 1954 Lyttleton Constitution. This opened the door to regional self-government in the East and West in 1957 and in the North in 1959 before full-blown independence was finally granted on 1 October 1960.

The British, meanwhile, obtained what they wanted. Understanding that independence was inevitable, the Foreign Office had drafted a paper to look into how 'we can sustain our position as a world power, particularly in the economic and strategic fields, against the dangers inherent in the present upsurge of nationalism' in order to 'maintain specific British interests on which [our] existence as a trading country depends', and it concluded that the challenge 'was to forestall nationalist demands which threaten our vital interests' by creating 'a class with a vested interest in co-operation' with the colonial power.[40]

Indeed, the small native elite had already demonstrated its penchant for the good life as far back as 1947. During a visit to London, British bureaucrats were shocked at the 'mountains of luggage' they had brought with them and their £2 a day hotel, causing George Padmore, the Trinidadian journalist and a leading pan-Africanist, to despair: 'There is a lot of fraud going on in the country, and many of us are exploiting the ignorance of the masses to line our pockets. Can't we try to be honest? A self-government, founded on fraud, deceit, and corruption, will not last.'[41] Later, in 1953, the town clerk of Norwich was engaged to conduct an enquiry into the Lagos Council: 'Running like a brightly coloured thread through the tangled skein of the Council's administration has been the subject of honesty or the lack of it – corruption. I could not get away from it at the public inquiry; it was mentioned in connection with almost every matter brought before me.'[42] Shortly afterwards, Wọlé Ṣóyínká, the future Nobel laureate then a student at Leeds, rushed down to London to meet with the representatives of the people only to discover that they appeared more intent on sleeping with master's daughter than liberating their constituents:

I recall one publicly humiliating instance: a revered national figure in a highly sensitive political position got so carried

40   Olakunle A. Lawal, 'From Colonial Reforms to Decolonization: Britain and the Transfer of Power in Nigeria, 1947–1960', *Journal of the Historical Society of Nigeria*, Vol. 19, 2010, 42.

41   Frederick Pilkington, 'The Problem of Unity in Nigeria', *African Affairs*, July 1956, Vol. 55, No. 220, 183.

42   Ibid., 187.

away with his date that he paid for a one-night stand with a cheque, at the bottom of which, just in case his scrawl was indecipherable, he had written his name, complete with his official position.

With increasing dismay, Ṣóyínká observed 'their preening, their ostentatious spending, and their cultivated condescension, even disdain, toward the people they were supposed to represent', and he feared the worst.[43]

Azikiwe himself was described by one colonial official as 'lazy' and 'out for money and women' following his interest in African Continental Bank, bought by him and his family in 1944 and recapitalised ten years later with money from the Eastern Region government he headed, in order to meet certain minimum requirements to remain in business:

> Such partisan action is a clearly dishonourable departure from the ethical conduct we are entitled to demand from people in Dr. Azikiwe's position . . . Zik wants money. Zik is a lazy man. Zik is not in anyway [sic] at all an ascetic nor in any way at all a man who believes that what he could do for Nigerians would be in Nigeria's own interests. Zik is motivated by one interest only: his own interest. And his own interest is money and the pleasure and power that money can buy.[44]

British administrators regarded Bello, the Sardauna of Sokoto, as 'far from an ideal party leader. He is vain and deplorably susceptible to flattery and his private life is disreputable to an extent that one day someone may blackmail

---

43 Wole Soyinka, *You Must Set Forth at Dawn: A Memoir*, New York: Random House, 2006, 42–3.

44 Pilkington, 'The Problem of Unity in Nigeria', 197–8.

him', but then it might be said that these were hostile witnesses. Azikiwe, for one, was immensely charismatic, as can be seen from the footage on his campaign for the 1979 presidency.[45] Only the teetotal Awólọ́wọ̀ appeared to escape such personal censure, but he was loathed because of his avowedly socialist views, brought back from his legal studies in the UK, where he witnessed first-hand Clement Attlee's post-war Labour government establish the National Health Service, make education up to age sixteen compulsory and build council houses for working people. Indeed, AG's 1954 manifesto was 'irrevocably committed to an ideology which places the interests of the masses first and invests in the state and public-owned corporations all the major means of production, distribution and exchange'.[46]

Under Awólọ́wọ̀'s watch, the Western Region was the first in the country to establish universal primary education, and the first in Africa to license a TV station. Cold War paranoia led the colonial authorities to ban all communist literature, forbid the appointment of known communists to the seven branches of the Nigerian public service and even seize the passport of the British-educated Samuel Ikoku, trade union leader and publisher of the *Nigerian Socialist Review*, who famously – and scandalously – defeated his own father in an election.

Each of the three dominant parties won majorities in their respective regions but the NPC won at the federal level by

45   Robert L. Tignor, 'Political Corruption in Nigeria before Independence', *Journal of Modern African Studies*, June 1993, Vol. 31, No. 2, June 1993, 175–202.

46   Quoted in John A. A. Ayoade, 'Party and Ideology in Nigeria: A Case Study of the Action Group', *Journal of Black Studies*, December 1985, Vol. 16, No. 2, 172.

teaming up with the NCNC, making Balewa the prime minister and Azikiwe the governor-general (à la Lord Lugard) until 1963, when the country voted to become a republic and he was transmuted into a ceremonial president. Awólọ́wọ̀, who saw himself as a national leader, appointed his deputy, Chief S. L. Akíntọ́lá, the former journalist who had praised Hubert Ògúndé, to head the Western House of Assembly while he concentrated on his bigger ambition. That wasn't to be realised, and Awólọ́wọ̀ would be remembered as 'the best president Nigeria never had'. Two years after his appointment, Akíntọ́lá broke with his mentor to align more closely with the NPC, in the hope of gaining greater access to resources at the federal level. Awólọ́wọ̀ then attempted to depose him, whereupon Balewa, seeking to gain a foothold in the region, declared a state of emergency and suspended the AG government for six months, at the end of which Akíntọ́lá was placed back in the premiership but under a new party. Awólọ́wọ̀ himself was subsequently charged with corruption and imprisoned, along with prominent members of his inner circle, found guilty of treasonable felony. One of them, Alhaji Lateef Jákàndè, who was to become a popular governor of Lagos State, wrote a 'studiously fair' account of what transpired at the time:

> Politics is a confused business much dependent upon money and involving the use of thugs by all parties as part of their normal political practice. We also see the shadier aspects of police procedure in obtaining evidence and questioning witnesses and there are hints of the supposed links between the presiding judge and the ruling political authorities.[47]

---

47 Martin Dent, 'Review of *The Trial of Chief Obafemi Awolowo* (1966)', *African Affairs*, July 1970, Vol. 69, No. 267, 300.

The following year matters deteriorated further following a census which saw a 70 percent increase in the populations of the Eastern and Western regions but only 30 percent in the Northern Region. The NPC government flatly refused to ratify the results and organised another census the following year, whereupon the Northern Region suddenly discovered eight million people it had previously overlooked, and more than the East and West combined, thereby giving it a clear numerical advantage at the federal level. This caused the AG and NCNC to come together at the 1964 federal elections, along with minority parties in what has become known as the Middle Belt, most of whose inhabitants were Christian and wary of northern domination despite the fact that they spoke Hausa. Things were especially tense in the Western Region, where Akíntọ́lá's party was seen as a symbol of the North's prepotence. Attempts to rig the election in favour of the status quo caused even Azikiwe, in a nationwide address, to call for secession if the results were not reversed:

> I make this suggestion because it is better for us and for our admirers abroad that we should disintegrate in peace and not in pieces. Should the politicians fail to heed this warning, then I will venture the prediction that the experience of the democratic [sic] Republic of the Congo will be child's play if it ever comes to our turn to play such a tragic role.[48]

Still more ironically, it was now the turn of the sultan of Sokoto, Bello, to respond that it was no longer possible to 'imagine a Nigeria that is composed of anything less than its present territory':

---

48 Douglas G. Anglin, 'Brinkmanship in Nigeria: The Federal Elections of 1964–65', *International Journal*, Spring 1965, 181.

I count the rivers of the Niger and Benue, the road, railway, and communications system, our openings to the outside world, the ports of Lagos and Apapa, and Kano airport. Each part of the country depends on the others for one service or another, and for one type of produce or another. Even the number of years we have been formally together have produced a great and wonderful unifying effect.[49]

Fresh elections had to be held the following year in both the Eastern and Western regions, but these quickly ran into the same problems amid accusations of multiple voting and stuffing of ballot boxes; in the words of Chief Rèmí Fàní-Káyòdé, the flamboyant deputy premier of the Western Region who narrowly escaped being killed in the unfolding events he helped bring about: 'Whether you vote for us or you don't, we are returning to office, we will make sure that invisible bodies vote for us if you refuse to. [We have] won the elections.'[50] In the event, both sides declared victory as people took to the streets, clashing with police and looting and burning the homes of Northern-favoured politicians, some of whom were killed. Balewa sent in the troops but to no avail. And then, in the early hours of 15 January 1966, junior army officers struck in what would be the first of the coups and attempted coups that would plague the country for the next three decades.

According to the BBC in the immediate aftermath, the coup was carried out by five Igbo majors who were 'open to Northern reprisals'. A follow-up editorial in the *Sunday Times of London* (23 January 1966) claimed that, 'According to reliable evidence, Major General Aguiyi–Ironsi, Head of

---

49   Tamuno, 'Separatist Agitations in Nigeria since 1914', 583.

50   Bola Ige, *People, Politics and Politicians of Nigeria, 1940–1979*, Ìbàdàn: Heinemann Educational Books, 1995, 277.

the Military Government, has a list of seventy further nota-
bles (apart from the Sarduna [sic] of Sokoto and the Prime
Minister) who have disappeared, largely Northern leaders.'[51]
Ahmadu Bello had been killed in his bedroom on the night
of the coup, alongside his senior wife and bodyguard as they
tried to shield him; Balewa's corpse was found at a roadside near Lagos a full six days later. In other words, the coup
was promptly interpreted as an Igbo-inspired move against
the Hausa-Fulani ruling class, which would have suited the
interests of the lately departed British, but in fact there
were eight majors involved, three of whom were Yorùbá,
as were two of the nine civilians killed (including Akíntọ́lá)
and two senior officers among the thirteen military and
police. Moreover, according to Major Adéwálé Adémóyèga,
one of the two Yorùbá coupists, 'There was no decision at
our meeting to single out any ethnic group for elimination.
Even those earmarked for arrest, four were northerners,
two were Westerners and two were Easterners.'[52] He also
asserted that their intentions were 'honourable', as did
Major Kaduna Nzeogwu (who became known as their
leader but actually joined when the coup was already in
full swing) over the radio:

> Our enemies are the political profiteers, swindlers, the men
> in high and low places that seek bribes and demand ten
> percent, those that seek to keep the country divided perma-
> nently so that they can remain in office as Ministers and
> VIPs of waste, the tribalists, the nepotists, those that make

---

51   Ngozika A. Obi-Ani and Paul Obi-Ani, 'January 15, 1966 Coup
d'État Reconsidered', *Nsukka Journal of the Humanities*, Vol. 24, No. 2,
2016, 21.

52   Adewale Ademoyega, *Why We Struck: The Story of the First
Nigerian Coup*, Ìbàdàn: Evans Brothers, 1981, 116.

the country big for nothing before international circles, those that have corrupted our society and put the Nigerian political calendar back by their words and deeds.[53]

In the event, loyalist troops swiftly overpowered the majors and their followers. The commanding officer, Major General Johnson Aguiyi-Ironsi, who also happened to be Igbo (raising suspicions that his accession was the whole point of the coup), told an emergency cabinet meeting of the surviving ministers that he couldn't guarantee the loyalty of the army unless power was immediately transferred to him. This was illegal in terms of the 1963 Republican Constitution, which provided for Balewa's deputy to take over and call for a state of emergency if need be, but perhaps the politicians simply panicked. Aguiyi-Ironsi forthwith suspended the federal and regional houses of assembly and promised a new, popular constitution preparatory to the soldiers returning to the barracks. However, Aguiyi-Ironsi was himself overthrown just seven months later in a counter-coup by northern soldiers, spearheaded by the twenty-eight-year-old Captain Theophilus Danjuma, who abducted him from Government House in Ìbàdàn, the capital of the Western Region, while the latter was on a tour and had him shot in the bush, along with his host, Lieutenant Colonel Adékúnlé Fájuyì, the military governor, who refused to leave his side (for which – like Jaja of Opobo – a statue was erected in his honour). As for Danjuma, he has long since numbered among the country's super-rich, having retired at forty-one to attend to his business affairs: according to

53 Speech broadcast over Radio Sokoto, midday, 15 January 1966; quoted in A.H.M. Kirk-Greene, *Crisis and Conflict in Nigeria: A Documentary Sourcebook, 1966–1969*, London: Oxford University Press, 1971, 126.

Forbes, he was worth US$750mn in 2015, courtesy of the oil wells he was awarded in the Niger Delta for services rendered.

The immediate cause of Aguiyi-Ironsi's downfall was his Unification Decree No. 34, a measure that abolished the federal structure and turned the regions into provinces. It didn't help that Aguiyi-Ironsi had failed to bring the coup plotters to trial, merely leaving them to languish in prison (and on half-salary!); he was also perceived to have accelerated the promotion of Igbo officers. To northerners already apprehensive of the large number of Igbo in their midst, mostly traders but also teachers and civil servants, the intention was to 'officialise their domination' of the region. Riots began in Kano in May 1966, with a demonstration by civil servants and students, and quickly spread to other cities. In all, 'several hundred' Igbo were killed, some of whom didn't help their cause by publicly displaying the famous picture in *Drum* magazine of a prostrate Bello under the boot of a triumphant Nzeogwu with the caption: 'I will not in future mix religion with politics,' a laudable and long overdue ambition, to be sure, but hardly politic under the circumstances. Significantly, northern soldiers refused to intervene when the police declared themselves unable to cope, a stance they repeated in the pogroms of September and October which resulted in about 10,000 Igbo dead.[54]

This was the signal for Lieutenant Colonel Odumegwu Ojukwu, the Igbo military governor of the Eastern Region, to call his people 'home'. It should be said, in this context, that he himself was smarting over the fact that the

---

54 This figure is taken from John de St. Jorre, *The Nigerian Civil War*, London: Hodder and Stroughton, 1972. However, some accounts claim three times this number.

architects of the counter-coup had installed his junior, Lieutenant Colonel Yakubu 'Jack' Gowon (aka Go On with One Nigeria), a Christian from the Middle Belt, as the more acceptable face of power, the same Gowon who in a radio broadcast declared himself 'very unhappy' about Easterners being 'killed and molested', acts that were now 'going beyond reason to the point of recklessness'. He also gloated over the fact that 'God, in his power, has entrusted the responsibility of this great country ... to the hands of another Northerner.' In amongst all this, it should be recalled that Gowon was only thirty-two years old at the time, in a country that was – and remains – a gerontocracy, as witness the incumbent and the two leading pretenders in 2023.[55] For his part, the equally youthful Ojukwu refused to acknowledge the authority of the new ruler and, after the collapse of the agreement he and Gowon brokered during last-ditch peace talks in neighbouring Ghana, proclaimed the independent state of Biafra.

According to the Aburi Accord, Ojukwu had proposed a 'drawing apart' of the regions because 'the separation of forces, the separation of the population is, in all sincerity, necessary in order to avoid further friction and further killings'. He further proposed that the head of the Federal Military Government would only implement unanimous decisions agreed upon by the regional heads, except for matters which affected the country as a whole, and he called for an end to the quota system in the military, which favoured northerners. Finally, Ojukwu, the chain-smoking, Oxford-educated son of Nigeria's first billionaire – who lent the new government his Rolls Royce to convey the lately departed Queen Elizabeth II to help us celebrate our

---

55   Radio Broadcast by Gowon, quoted in Wole Soyinka, *The Man Died*, London: Rex Collings, 1972, 119–20.

'independence' – proposed 31 March 1967 as the deadline
for implementing what was agreed upon. Back in Lagos,
however, it was deemed that Gowon had conceded too
much, that, in the words of the horrified permanent secretary in the civil service, Prince Solomon Akenzua (a
descendant of the deposed oba of Benin who was himself
to soon inherit the crown, albeit without the divine powers),
complained that Gowon had 'legalized' regionalism, which
'would make the country very weak' and ultimately lead to
its disintegration. The stalemate persisted for four months
as Ojukwu single-handedly implemented the agreement by
seizing all federal revenue in 'his' part of the country,
whereupon, on 27 May, Gowon declared a state of emergency across the entire country and assumed 'full powers
for the short period necessary to carry out the measures
which were now urgently required'. He also announced the
creation of twelve states to replace the regions. The Eastern
Region was broken into three states, thereby giving the Igbo
a majority in only one state and bringing on board the
'minorities' in the other two. Furious, on 30 May Ojukwu
proclaimed that 'the territory and Region known as Eastern
Nigeria, together with her continental shelves and territorial waters, shall henceforth be an independent sovereign
state of the name and title, the Republic of Biafra'. Nothing
much happened for another thirty days as the government
seemed to drift, but on 6 July Gowon announced a 'police
action' which quickly descended into civil war.[56]

The war, which Gowon optimistically forecast would last
no more than four to eight weeks, dragged on for thirty
months (from 6 July 1967 to 15 January 1970), helping to

---

56 Ayomide Akinbode, 'Aburi Accord: What Really Happened in
Ghana in 1967 that led to the Nigerian Civil War?', *HistoryVille*, 4
January 2021.

entrench military rule by allowing the institution to promote itself as the saviour of the country, although the actual day-to-day administration was largely in the hands of Awólọ́wọ̀, who was released from prison to become Gowon's deputy in the National Executive Council, as well as commissioner for finance. This was a smart move, not only because it kept the Yorùbá onside but also because Awólọ́wọ̀ had already proven himself a first-rate administrator in the Western Region, where he had balanced the budget for six consecutive years, and he did the same this time around: Nigeria prosecuted the war without indebting itself to the global financial institutions from which we now borrow in order to pay government salaries. Nevertheless, Gowon's ascendancy, courtesy of the same Western Region where northern machinations led to the coup in the first place, effectively meant that the Nigerian military was pressed into service as the surrogate of northern power at the same time it began the process of transmuting itself into a political player in its own right. One of its first tasks was to reverse the previous 'imbalance' that saw a preponderance of southern officers able to strike in the very bedroom of the northern establishment.

The only wonder about Biafra was that it held out as long as it did, testimony to the spirit that motivated the secession. Up to two million perished, mostly by starvation, and deliberately so; as Awólọ́wọ̀ is said to have commented: 'All is fair in war, and starvation is one of the weapons of war. I don't see why we should feed our enemies fat in order for them to fight harder.'[57] By September 1968, the Red Cross reported between 8,000 and 10,000 deaths a day.[58]

---

57 Chinua Achebe, *There Was a Country: A Personal History of Biafra*, London: Penguin, 2012, 33.

58 'Deaths in Biafra put at 8,000 a day', *New York Times*, 28 September 1968.

Tragically, it was easy enough to blockade Biafra because, as I observe in the preface to this book, the world was wedded to the status quo of pre-determined colonial boundaries, although many 'ordinary' people were on the side of the underdog in the first armed conflict to be widely televised, with Don McCullin's photograph of an emaciated albino boy one of the century's iconic images; as McCullin remarked: 'To be a starving Biafran orphan was to be in a most pitiable situation, but to be a starving albino Biafran was to be in a position beyond description. Dying of starvation, he was still among his peers an object of ostracism, ridicule and insult.' There was also the 12 July 1968 cover of *Life* magazine, 'Starving Children of Biafra War', now available on eBay at US$14.95: 'great for framing'. Meanwhile, John Lennon returned his MBE to the (recently departed) Queen, and Martin Amis, then at university, was shocked to encounter 'an incredible reactionary' who supported not only '*Nigeria* vs Biafra' (his italics) but the Soviet Union's occupation of Czechoslovakia.[59] And at a rally in New York in September that same year, Rabbi Marc H. Tanenbaum, chair of the Interreligious Liaison Committee for Biafran Relief, explicitly compared the plight of Biafrans to that of the Jews in Nazi Germany only a quarter-century before.

In all this, it is telling that there has yet to be an official account of the most significant event in our short history, although there have been any number of poems, short stories, novels and memoirs, which seems fitting given what I regard as the fictional nature of the country itself. But there was nothing fictional about the suffering, exemplified at the very start by the notorious events at Asaba, in what was previously part of the old Western Region but just

---

59 Martin Amis, *Experience*, London: Vintage, 2001, 213.

across the Niger River in the putative Biafra. Just four months into the conflict, on 5 October 1967, federal troops entered the town in pursuit of Biafran soldiers, who had retreated across the bridge back to Onitsha in the by now real Biafra. Claiming that the locals were enemy sympathisers, soldiers under the command of General Murtala Muhammad, 'a fire-breathing 28-year-old Northerner whose dislike of Ibos has never been disguised'[60] (and after whom the international airport in Lagos is named), bared their fangs:

> As troops took control of the town, groups of soldiers went from house to house looting, raping, rounding up boys and men accused of being Biafran sympathizers, and demanding money from those who were spared ... Males who had been singled out were either shot on the spot or taken to the police station on Nnebisi Road (Asaba's main street), the High Court on the Okpanam road, the soccer field, or the riverbank, where they were executed. Witnesses remember seeing the streets littered with corpses. Many families fled, while others hid in the ceilings of their houses.[61]

Attempting to appease the troops, the chiefs decided to raise a levy of £50 from each of the town's five quarters, together with an initial donation of £50 to pay for drinks, which was immediately delivered to one of the officers, who in turn expressed regret at the number killed from 'stray bullets'.[62]

---

60 Alfred Friendly Jr., 'A City Shows Scars of the Nigerian War', *New York Times*, 26 September 1967.

61 S. Elizabeth Bird and Fraser Ottanelli, 'The History and Legacy of the Asaba, Nigeria', *African Studies Review*, Vol. 54, No. 3, December 2011, Vol. 54, No. 3, 8.

62 Ibid., 10.

Early the next morning, four men were despatched to deliver their contribution but never returned. A second group also disappeared. That evening, the chiefs ordered town criers to summon everyone to assemble the next day to welcome the federal troops and offer a pledge of loyalty to 'One Nigeria' (although there was a great deal of scepticism, with some even refusing to join):

> Up to four thousand townspeople participated. Many gathered by a large tree on Nnebisi Road, where they were joined by groups coming out from houses throughout the five quarters of Asaba. With many singing, dancing, and chanting 'One Nigeria,' they advanced past St. Joseph's Church and continued east. Any expectation that these gestures of goodwill would appease the troops was quickly dashed. Marchers were flanked by federal soldiers to prevent them from fleeing, and witnesses report that the soldiers also selected males at random and executed them in full view of participants. Survivors recalled seeing dozens of bodies, including that of one of the town criers, along with the mangled bodies of the four who had been sent earlier to deliver money.[63]

The marchers continued. Once they reached the corner of Ogbogonogo and Ogbeke markets, 'women and small children were corralled into the maternity hospital on Nnebisi Road, while the men were channelled between two rows of soldiers down the side road that led to the square at Ogbeosowa', whereupon 'machine guns, both mounted on trucks and free-standing, were revealed, and mass shooting began'. In the words of an eyewitness:

---

63   Ibid., 11.

Some people broke loose and tried to run away. My brother was holding me by the hand; he released me and pushed me further into the crowd . . . They shot my brother in the back, he fell down, and I saw blood coming out of his body. And then the rest of us . . . just fell down on top of each other. And they continued shooting, and shooting, and shooting . . . I lost count of time, I don't know how long it took . . . After some time there was silence. I stood up . . . my body was covered in blood, but I knew that I was safe. My father was lying not far away; his eyes were open but he was dead.[64]

The shooting continued for several hours until darkness began to fall. The survivors lay still under the heap of the dead and dying until they felt it was safe to wriggle out from under and flee into the nearby bush. In the absence of the men, it fell to the women to bury the corpses, mostly in shallow graves, some just thrown into the Niger River. In all, up to 1,000 were killed, about a tenth of the population.

The soldiers remained in Asaba while they waited to cross the river. Some were billeted in the houses of families whose sons and husbands they had killed. Individual acts of rape were commonplace. An eyewitness told of one young woman who was abducted by soldiers and held for a week before she was returned to her father: 'When she came back, she was a different girl . . . She wouldn't talk to anybody, she was very weepy . . . You see, we come from a culture . . . where talk like rape is taboo, you know, a girl says she's been raped, getting married is like an impossibility.'[65]

---

64 Ibid., 10–11.
65 Ibid., 13.

The government did its best to censor the event and for good reason:

> In the oral accounts of what happened, a consistent theme is outrage at a despicable betrayal; the people of Asaba had assembled to declare allegiance to Nigeria in a traditional display of dance and music, only to be slaughtered. And thus this news sent a uniquely chilling message to other Igbo in Biafra, effectively helping prolong the war.[66]

Since then, there has been a concerted effort by interested parties to make what happened in Asaba better known. As of this writing, the Asaba Memorial Committee under Chief Chuck Nduka-Eze, the Isama Ajie of Asaba, is organising an art exhibition as 'part of a series of remembrance activities to support the development of a permanent physical space – a world-class nature park, monument, artistic and cultural centre in honour of all those who lost their lives and were displaced by the Asaba massacre'. The Memorial Park 'will have, as its foundation, 1,000 trees as a symbol of all the lives lost. It will be a legacy project that finally gives homage to the victims, their families and becomes a place for reflection on healing for Asabans and all Nigerians.'

Ojukwu fled to Côte d'Ivoire (one of the five countries to recognise Biafra, along with Gabon, Haiti, Tanzania and Zambia) just ahead of the federal troops, despite his earlier vow to die on the battlefield because, in his words, 'Whilst I live, Biafra lives. If I am no more, it would only be a matter of time for the noble concept to be sent into oblivion.' Philip Effiong, the deputy he handed over the reins of power to, was not fooled by this display of megalomania

---

66 Ibid., 19.

that would equate the 'noble concept' with Ojukwu's own presumably noble self: 'Those elements of the old government regime who have made negotiation and reconciliation impossible have removed themselves from the scene,' as Effiong wrote in his memoir. He returned to Nigeria a decade later 'with pomp, married an ex-beauty queen, and was given a burial with full military honours after he died in 2011', having unsuccessfully run for the presidency – of Nigeria! – in 2003 and 2007.[67]

---

67 Emmanuel Iduma, *I Am Still with You: A Reckoning with Silence, Inheritance and History*, London: William Collins, 2023, 86.

3

Perpetual War; or, Soja Come, Soja Go[1]

The doctor told him I was having psychiatric problems. I said yes, I must be, because all I can see on the benches are kangaroos.

– Ken Saro-Wiwa

How animal go know say dem no born me as slave? / How animal go know say slave trade don pass? / And they wan dash us human rights / Animal must talk to human beings / Give dem human rights.

– Fẹlá Kútì

Following the end of the civil war, Gowon declared a 'No Victor No Vanquished' policy. This immediately won him plaudits from the international community – even earning him comparison with Abraham Lincoln – but the former Biafrans took a different view when he also announced they would be given only £20 each in the new currency, irrespective of their previous bank balance in their now worthless Biafran pounds. At the same time, he promulgated the Indigenisation Decree, forcing foreign companies to sell a percentage of their shares to Nigerians, thereby

---

1 'Soja come, soja go' (meaning 'solider come, soldier go') is from a song by Fela Kuti lamenting the incessant rotation of power among the army generals from the civil war until they were finally forced to civilian rule in 1999.

benefiting the mainly Hausa and Yorùbá elites while robbing the now impoverished Igbo of the same opportunity. But there was little they could do. The ever-smiling (and genuinely modest) youngest African head of state rode high on his victory, assisted by the oil boom which followed in its wake. Revenue from petroleum rose exponentially from ₦166mn in 1970 to ₦3.7bn just four years later, when Arab producers embargoed oil following Israel's 1973 attack on Egypt, causing Gowon to quip that the country's problem was not money but how to spend it, a remark he hasn't been allowed to forget (and rightly so). Unfortunately, the sudden boom was also his undoing as the country became mired in the corruption for which it has become justly famous, most notoriously in 1975 when 400 cargo ships carrying 1.5 million tons of cement clogged the Lagos harbour even as they accrued demurrage. Worse yet, spoiled and inferior-grade product was deliberately mixed up with the cement by unscrupulous importers who knew the score, leading to the phenomenon of collapsed buildings, which hasn't abated since.

Gowon also pledged to transfer power to an elected civilian government, but in 1974, heeding the call of 'a large number of well-meaning and responsible Nigerians from all walks of life', he considered that it would be 'utterly irresponsible [of him] to leave the nation in the lurch by a precipitate withdrawal which will certainly throw the nation back into confusion' and announced his intention to stay put indefinitely.[2] The following year, while

---

2 'National Day Broadcast by Gen. Yakubu Gowon, Head of the Federal Military Government and Commander-in-Chief of the Armed Forces', Oct. 1, 1974; quoted in Pita Ogaba and George Klay Kieh, 'Military Disengagement from African Politics: The Nigerian Experience', *Africa Spectrum*, Vol. 27, No. 1, 1992, 21.

attending an Organisation of African Unity meeting in Kampala, Uganda, he was informed by his host, President Idi Amin Dada, that he had been overthrown in a bloodless coup by his chief of staff, and that his deputy, General Murtala Muhammed (he of the Asaba massacres) had taken over. Murtala survived just seven months before he was assassinated in a botched coup attempt by rogue elements of an already conflicted army (his bullet-ridden Mercedes Benz is an exhibit at the National Museum in Lagos), whereupon Olúṣẹ́gun Ọbásanjọ́, his deputy, was prevailed upon 'against my personal wish and desire' to see through the transition to civilian rule initiated by his slain mentor.

Ọbásanjọ́ earned considerable international respect as the first Nigerian soldier to hand over power to an elected civilian administration when he installed Alhaji Shehu Shagari, a northerner, as president of the Second Republic on 1 October 1979. More sceptical Nigerians believe that he had little choice and was all along teleguided by his northern 'masters', hence the need to give his 'minder', Major General Musa Yar'Adua, a member of the Fulani aristocracy, a double promotion in order to become his second-in-command. There was also the matter of the controversial ruling by the attorney general concerning Shagari's victory. Foreshadowing the 2023 elections, the electoral commission had earlier stipulated that only the candidate who won not less than 25 percent of the votes in at least two-thirds of the then nineteen states (seven new ones had been created in 1976) could be declared the outright winner. As it turned out, Shagari claimed the most votes – 5,688,857 – but won the required percentage in only twelve states, one less than he needed. Awólọ́wọ̀, the closest of his four rivals (which also included Azikiwe), polled 4,916,651, capturing six states in the process.

According to the commission's own rules, there should have been a run-off, but the commission's chairperson as well as the attorney general and minister of justice decided that Shagari had won in '12 two-third States' despite the fact that the commission had only registered the parties on the basis that they had working offices in at least thirteen states. Ọbásanjọ himself refused to intervene, protesting the commission's independence. Awólọ́wọ̀ took the matter to the Supreme Court, which ruled in Shagari's favour but, curiously, added that its judgment in this case should not be taken as a precedent.

The Second Republic soon became a byword for corruption on a grand scale, fuelled by the spike in oil prices following the 1979 Iranian Revolution, a bonanza that ended any notion of the North's wanting to secede. Indeed, so anxious was the ruling elite to control this apparently inexhaustible dowry that in 1978 it passed the Land Use Decree. This act vested all land in the 'military governor' of the state, with individuals possessing only the right of occupancy, revocable at any time in the 'overriding public interest', notably 'for mining purposes or oil pipelines or any other purpose connected therewith':

In essence, the inhabitants of the region may be dispossessed of their land whenever their land is required for oil exploration, making them tenants-at-will of the oil industry on land they have owned and inhabited for centuries. The Act thus complemented and completed the intent of previous legislation to grant the federal government exclusive ownership and control of oil resources.[3]

---

3 Rhuks T. Ako, 'Nigeria's Land Use Act: An Anti-Thesis to Environmental Justice', *Journal of African Law*, Vol. 53, No. 2, 2009, 9.

Furthermore:

> In addition to depriving the host communities of certainty
> in land rights, the Act was instrumental in depriving these
> communities from owning land within the region. Land in
> the oil-rich region was appropriated for the benefit of oil
> companies, government officials and their cronies to the
> detriment of the original (traditional) landholders ...
> Thereafter, the region became a land speculators' paradise,
> driving up the economic value of land beyond the reach of
> its local population. The influx of these 'foreign' land spec-
> ulators who purchased land and or resold it to oil companies
> circumvented the involvement of local communities in the
> management of land within the Niger Delta. This helped to
> deprive them of subsequent pecuniary benefits in the form
> of rent and participation in the decision-making process on
> land use and compensation, and further deepened poverty
> in the region.[4]

When the military finally stepped aside after thirteen years,
the decree was incorporated into the 1979 Constitution
(and, later, the 1999 Constitution) as one of four enact-
ments that couldn't be invalidated by the provisions of the
constitution itself. This, together with another provision
vesting 'control of all minerals, mineral oil and natural gas
in, under or upon any land in Nigeria ... in the Government of the Federation', deprived the communities in the
Niger Delta of any rights to a commodity that was shortly
to finance a brand-new capital, even as it polluted their
farms and rivers, destroying the traditional bases of their
economy.

---

4   Ibid., 10.

It was a measure of Shagari's first, four-year term that Nigeria earned over US$40bn in oil receipts but took on external debts of over US$12bn, a great deal of which went into the foreign accounts of party cronies. One of them, Shagari's campaign manager Umaru Dikko, who became minister of transport and head of the presidential task force on rice, supposedly said there was no poverty in Nigeria because people 'had not reached the point of eating from dustbins'. Addicted to easy money, Dikko and his cohorts ensured that an unpopular and ineffectual Shagari more than doubled his votes in the 1983 election, in the process teaching their 1965 predecessors a lesson in election rigging. In one famous instance, the ruling NPN won by a margin greater than the population of the state, as announced on the national radio network of a neighbouring country even as the ballot boxes were being collected from the polling centres. As it happened, the party had lost heavily to Awólọ́wọ̀ in 1979 in that same state, Oǹdó, it being part of his ethnic 'territory'. Small wonder that the populace cheered the soldiers when they made a comeback on the last day of the year, not least by releasing Dikko's rice from the warehouses where he had stored it the better to raise the price; what the populace didn't know, but was soon to discover, was that the military as an institution had become addicted to power, and part of this addiction necessarily entailed wholesale contempt for the 'bloody civilians' (the military's own terminology), who had to be whipped into line.

The evidence was already there. Consider the 1973 case of Minere Amakiri, the Rivers State journalist who had his head shaved with a broken bottle (or was it a rusty blade?) and then received twenty-four lashes, 'howling in excruciating pain', for writing about an impending teachers' strike over non-payment of salaries. The military governor,

Commodore (now King) Alfred Diete-Spiff, who was cele-
brating his thirty-fourth birthday, found the story
'embarrassing'. The assault at the party took place at Government Lodge, in the pouring rain and in full view of the
governor's guests. Amakiri was subsequently awarded
damages in a case fought on his behalf by Gani Fáwèhinmi,
the late social crusader, which made him more fortunate
than Fęlá Kútì, whose house in Lagos was burnt to the
ground in February 1977 by 1,000 soldiers from the nearby
barracks on the orders of General Ọbásanjọ́. Fęlá's offence
was to have disparaged soldiers in one of his songs,
'Zombie': 'Zombie no go go until you tell am to go, Zombie
no go think unless you tell am to think, Zombie no go turn
until you tell am to turn, Go and kill, Go and die, Go and
quench, Halt!'

The military's act of wanton destruction – in the course
of which Fęlá's elderly mother, who had once led the women
of Abẹ̀òkúta against the colonial power, was thrown from a
first-floor balcony (and was later to die as a result of the
injuries) – caused sufficient disquiet among the general
populace for the government to convene a tribunal to
investigate the circumstances surrounding the episode.
Despite overwhelming proof of premeditation by the army,
including eyewitness accounts of soldiers carrying jerry-
cans of petrol and complaints by the fire brigade that they
were prevented from entering the area, the tribunal concluded that the fire was started by 'an exasperated and
unknown soldier'. The tribunal also held that Fęlá had
been deliberately provocative by calling his house a republic: 'Government wishes to point out that no single
individual, no matter how powerful or popular, can set
himself above the laws of the land and the government will
not allow or tolerate the existence of a situation which is
capable of undermining the very basis of civilised society.'

Fẹlá subsequently sued the authorities but the case was thrown out on the grounds that 'government can do no wrong', the enduring principle of military rule, as the people of Myanmar have been lately rediscovering. As a final insult, the site of the destroyed property was seized because, the authorities argued, Fẹlá and the army couldn't co-exist within the same vicinity, in the process revealing its ultimate impotence against Abàmì Ẹ̀dá, the strange one, armed only with his music.

The habit of physically brutalising 'unruly' citizens is deeply embedded in Nigerian military culture and was perfectly exemplified by the incoming regime of Major General Muhammadu Buhari and his deputy, Major General Túndé Ìdíàgbọn. One of their first acts was to launch what they were pleased to call a War Against Indiscipline which saw grown men and women publicly flogged in the streets by battle-ready soldiers for pissing in the open gutter or for not queuing at the bus stop. This even as their Cuban counterparts, without our abundant crude oil and with their US neighbour breathing down their neck, waged a struggle against South Africa in nearby Angola that began to unravel the apartheid we were fighting 'with ordinary mouth', as the saying goes. The Buhari junta also proscribed the Nigerian Medical Association and the National Association of Nigerian Students (in the days when the latter was truly radical), and it enacted Public Officers (Protection against False Accusation) Decree No. 4, making it an offence for a newspaper to publish any information, whether true or not, which could bring the government or a government official into ridicule or disrepute. If convicted, the publishing house concerned could be proscribed and the erring journalists imprisoned for up to two years. Two such, Túndé Thompson and Nduka Irabor, both of the *Guardian* (then the country's best daily by far), were promptly dragged before the tribunal in June 1984 and given one year each for an exclusive report on the new heads of diplomatic missions, even though the government admitted in the course of the trial that the report was substantially true.

Worse again was the State Security (Detention of Persons) Decree No. 2 of 1984, which allowed for three months renewable detention at the sole discretion of Ìdíàgbọn:

> If the Chief of Staff, Supreme Headquarters, is satisfied that any person is or has recently been concerned in acts prejudicial to state security or has contributed to the economic adversity of the nation or in the perpetration or instigation of such acts, and that by reason thereof it is necessary to exercise control over him, he may by order in writing direct that that person be detained in civil prison or police station or such other place specified by him.

Most egregious of all was Decree 20, which allowed the execution of three men – Lawal Ojúọlápé (thirty), Bartholomew Owoh (twenty-six) and Bernard Ògèdeṅgbé (twenty-nine) – for crimes they had been convicted of but which hadn't carried the death sentence at the time they had committed them. This caused huge outrage both at home and abroad, but Buhari went ahead anyway. Later, while contesting the 2007 presidential election, he was asked if he had second thoughts about what he had done, but he 'declared in the most categorical terms that he has no regrets over this murder and would do so again'.[5]

The regime, impervious to all reason, lasted just twenty months before it was overthrown by General Ibrahim

---

5 Wole Soyinka, 'The crimes of Buhari', *Sahara Reporters*, 15 January 2007.

Babangida in August 1985. Babangida courted popularity by repealing Decree No. 4, releasing Thompson and Irabor and promising an early return to civil democratic rule (any discussion of which had been prohibited by Buhari), but he didn't repeal Decree 2; on the contrary, he doubled the period of detention from three to six months and extended the authority to invoke it to the Ministry of the Interior, in addition to the military and the police. Towards the end of his tenure, it was said that pre-signed detention orders – just fill in the name – were piled high on the attorney general's desk, but that was later, after the country had woken up to the real face of the man the press was eventually to dub the 'evil genius'.

Initially, Babangida's administration appeared receptive to dialogue, prompting even Wọlé Ṣóyínká to call it a 'listening government' before turning on the president for practicing 'voodoo-type democracy', but Babangida's eight-year tenure was to prove more wasteful than any before it. According to the World Bank, 'There was a breakdown in fiscal and monetary discipline during 1990.' A subsequent panel in 1994 reported that US$12.4bn accruing from oil sales, including the temporary windfall from the 1990 Gulf crisis, were unaccounted for. All that money went through special dedicated accounts controlled directly from the presidency, 'by-passing budgetary mechanisms of expenditure authorization and control'. To that end, Babangida promulgated the Central Bank of Nigeria Decree No. 24 of 1991, empowering him to 'direct' the bank 'as to the monetary and banking policy pursued or intended to be pursued', policy that would be 'binding'. Many believe that Babangida personally stole US$4bn of that money; some of the rest went to seventy six-door Mercedes Benz limousines for visiting heads of state when Nigeria hosted the 1991 Organisation of African Unity jamboree.

The Babangida regime also began the practice of assassinating awkward voices, when Délé Gíwá, editor-in-chief of the weekly *Newswatch* magazine, was killed by a parcel bomb delivered to his house late in the morning on Sunday, 9 October 1986. The murder has remained unsolved but events leading up to it point to Babangida himself. Only three days earlier, Gíwá was invited to the headquarters of the State Security Service and presented with allegations that he was fomenting a socialist revolution. Suitably shocked, he said to Ray Ekpu, one of his associates, 'If they can think this of me, then I am not safe. They are only trying to give a dog a bad name in order to hang it.'[6] He also reported the matter to his lawyer, Gani Fáwẹ̀hinmi, who had been contacted by phone by the director of military intelligence, Colonel Halilu Akilu, two days before asking for directions to Gíwá's house. Later rumours claimed that Gíwá had been working on a story implicating Babangida and his wife in drug smuggling, for which the country was just then becoming notorious. However, Babangida's lasting contribution to Nigeria's evolving political history was the annulment of the 12 June 1993 presidential election before the counting was over, but not before Chief Moshood Abíọ́lá, the flamboyant billionaire businessman, had emerged the clear winner. Worse yet, the annulment itself came at the end of a messy transition-to-civil-rule programme that many were beginning to think would never end. Little did we know!

The programme kicked off in January 1986 with the inauguration of a seventeen-member Political Bureau tasked with suggesting ways of solving the country's political problems and reviewing past constitutions with a view to

---

6 Onukaba Ojo and Dele Olojede, *Born to Run*, Ìbàdàn: Spectrum Books, 1989, 173.

fashioning a new one. On that occasion, Babangida also promised to leave office on 1 October 1990. In July 1987, he announced a new transition timetable which would end two years later than previously anticipated. The following September, he inaugurated a forty-five-member Constitutional Review Commission which submitted its report in March 1988, whereupon Babangida convened a Constituent Assembly to review the draft constitution produced by the Commission.

The new constitution was promulgated in May 1989, to come into effect with the Third Republic on 1 October 1992. Meanwhile, the electoral commission registered thirteen (out of about forty) political parties, but in October Babangida suddenly dissolved all of them on the grounds that they lacked distinctive ideologies and were in any case full of discredited – 'old breed' – politicians. He proceeded to create two new parties – one 'a little bit to the left', the other 'a little bit to the right' – whose manifestoes and constitutions he wrote. In pre-emptively annulling the 1993 election, Babangida cited electoral irregularities, yet the voting system he adopted resulted in what many agree were the freest and fairest elections ever held in the country. Under the Open–Secret Ballot System, voters were required to stand behind the portrait of their chosen candidate. They were counted there and then and the results announced, recorded and signed off by the party agents. Although crude, even 'primitive' (according to a former attorney general), this was generally seen as appropriate in so far as it reduced the possibility of rigging. Unfortunately, many people were victimised after they were publicly seen to be supporting the 'wrong' candidate, for instance tenants suddenly finding their belongings in the street.

Babangida himself tried to cling on to power amid waves of protests until he was forced to resign on 26 August, leaving behind an 'interim' government headed Ernest Shónẹ̀-kàn, a lacklustre businessman with no previous political experience, along with General Sani Abacha, Babangida's former deputy and long-time fellow coup plotter, whose role was to help 'stabilise' this unlikely contraption. Babangida hasn't since cared to give an explanation – much less an apology – for the trauma he caused the nation by this singular act of hubris; it is the question every journalist asks him but which he studiously ducks, offering instead that he did it because Abíọ́lá and the people around him didn't help matters; that he would have flooded Aso Rock with his Yorùbá ethnic group; that he would have made a 'lousy President' and would, in any case, have been overthrown by Abacha within six months. But if he believed this last to be true, why did he fail to retire the general along with the rest of the high command? Because he was 'being loyal to a friend'; not only that, but junior officers might have stepped into the breach, and 'I knew that this country could not afford the luxury of having lieutenant colonels and below as leaders.'[7] As if acting to script, Abacha gave Shónẹ̀kàn's government just three months before pushing it aside (that is, before telling Shónẹ̀kàn not to bother coming to the office today), helped along by a Lagos High Court ruling declaring the government illegal since the decree establishing it had been signed after Babangida left office, such was the concern with due process.

Abacha, who knew he had to appease both local and international opinion in order to garner credibility, immediately stressed 'the unflinching commitment of this Administration to an early return to civil democratic rule', to which end he embarked straightaway on his own tortured

---

7   Adewale Maja-Pearce, 'Army Arrangement', *London Review of Books*, Vol. 21, No. 7, 1 April 1999.

transition programme by convening yet another conference to write yet another constitution guaranteeing 'an enduring democracy' as well as determine the date of his exit from power; 'tortured' not only because his predecessor had just recently shelled out US$52mn for the now botched Third Republic, but because 'an early return to civil democratic' rule could have been achieved much more quickly – and far more cheaply – by simply de-annulling the annulment and allowing Abíọlá to assume his mandate, but in this he was assisted in true Nigerian fashion by would-be delegates to yet another conference, who besieged him even before he finished stating the terms.

Abíọlá, for his part, hardly helped his cause, and not only because he believed in the promises of an infantry general who had announced both the 1983 and 1985 coups. His political naiveté was already apparent in his initial reaction to the annulment, which was to flee the country – through the international airport! – and proceed to give extensive interviews to the foreign media while his supporters died on the streets. He justified his action on the grounds that he didn't want to be assassinated, but then this unlikely hero was himself part of 'the problem with Nigeria', having made the fabulous wealth that he had used to win the elections by not fulfilling telecommunication contracts awarded by the same military that was now shafting him. Some say that he was the main sponsor of Babangida's 1985 coup because the Buhari/Ìdíàgbọn regime wasn't playing ball, but that, too, is another story. One year later, when the hapless chief of 140 titles (and almost as many wives) rediscovered his mandate at a rally in Lagos, he was promptly locked up for treason and remained so for the rest of Abacha's tenure, only to die one month after his nemesis passed away, apparently – à la Jaja of Opobo – from drinking poisoned tea, although the autopsy claimed he succumbed to 'massive heart failure'.

The list of civilians who served under our latest 'animal in human skin' and gave his administration a veneer of respectability was long and contained some distinguished names, including Alhaji Baba Gana Kingibe, Abíọ́lá's running mate, who became minister for external affairs; Alex Ibru, publisher of the *Guardian*, who became minister for internal affairs; Alhaji Lateef Jákàńdè, former acolyte of Awólọ́wọ̀ and sometime civilian governor of Lagos State, who became minister for works and housing; and Dr Olú Onàgorúwà, a constitutional lawyer of otherwise impeccable credentials (so what's new?), who became attorney general and minister for justice. Of these, only Kingibe was from the northern aristocracy. All the others were southerners, and all of them got their comeuppance when Abacha judged that he could dispense with them.

Ibru was the first to go when his newspaper group was proscribed in August 1994 for an article which claimed that there was a split in the Provisional Ruling Council between the hawks and the doves, insofar as these terms mean anything in a military junta. Onàgorúwà followed a month later when he disowned the decrees proscribing Guardian Newspapers Ltd. and two others – Abíọ́lá's Concord Newspapers and *African Concord* weekly magazine, and Punch Newspapers Ltd. – as the handiwork of 'certain bureaucratic and political forces'. A few months after his departure, Ibru was the victim of an assassination attempt when unidentified gunmen drew alongside his car on a busy Lagos expressway in the middle of the day and let loose a volley of shots. He survived and fled to London, where he remained until Abacha's demise. Onàgorúwà fared less well. His eldest son was shot dead – also by unidentified gunmen – outside his front door as he was getting out of his car. Onàgorúwà subsequently went on record accusing Abacha of ordering the murder and Alhaji Ibrahim Coomassie, the inspector general of police, of covering it up – but only after Abacha himself was safely dead.[8]

Next in line were General Ọbásanjọ́ and his former deputy, Major General Musa Yar'Adua, both of whom were dragged before a secret military tribunal and accused of fomenting a coup. Also arrested on the same charges were four journalists – Kúnlé Ajíbádé, Chris Anyanwu, Ben-Charles Obi and George Mbah – and a human rights activist, Dr Bẹ́kọ̀ Ransome-Kútì, brother of Fẹlá. All were given twenty-five years (later reduced to fifteen), except Yar'Adua, who was sentenced to death. His crime was to have enjoined Abacha's constitutional conference to set a date – 1 January 1996 – for the final termination of military rule, in defiance of Abacha's self-succession plan, which by then was becoming increasingly obvious. It was testimony to Yar'Adua's position within the Hausa-Fulani aristocracy that the sentence was subsequently commuted to life, although many believe that Abacha, who caused a number of prominent people to be murdered (of which more presently), allowed him to die in prison of an undisclosed ailment in November 1997; but the beastly nature of the regime had already been revealed by the judicial murders of Ken Saro-Wiwa and eight of his fellow environmental activists on 10 November 1995.

---

8 'I think Coomassie . . . has been exerting pressure on [his officers] not to do their job. Coomassie knows my son's killers . . . He was acting in league with Abacha. Whenever there was an atrocious murder or assassination, Coomassie will go and arrest the friends and relatives of the victims.' *Tell*, 28 December 1998.

Ken Saro-Wiwa was a member of the million plus Ogoni ethnic group in Rivers State, a minority even among the minorities but one whose oil contributed over US$30bn to the national coffers between 1958 and 1992, the year the oil companies were forced to withdraw following the activities of Saro-Wiwa's Movement for the Survival of the Ogoni People (MOSOP). Saro-Wiwa claimed to have founded MOSOP following a 'Voice' he heard late one night in 1989 as he worked alone in his study in Port Harcourt, an event he describes in *My Story*, the 10,000-word statement he was prevented from reading at the tribunal that was about to hang him. The Voice told him to put his abilities and resources 'so carefully nurtured over the years' at the service of his people, and it assured him of success in his lifetime 'or thereafter' but also warned him of 'the great risks' he would be running. Without hesitation, he said, he accepted the challenge and received his family's 'full understanding' when he told them 'of the cause to which I was about to dedicate my life'.

It happened that I first met Saro-Wiwa shortly after his conversion and it should be said that he did come across as inflated with his self-proclaimed role as the 'prophet', the 'keeper of the conscience of society', and the 'protector of the Ogoni', as he never tired of reminding anyone who cared to listen. At the time, I was editor of the (now defunct) Heinemann African Writers Series and he wanted an 'international' outlet for some of his self-published books. He wrote in all genres but we only handled fiction and poetry, so he gave me a collection of short stories along with a novel about the civil war written in what he called 'rotten English', which is to say English as we dey talk am for Naija, otherwise derogatorily called 'pidgin' or 'broken'. I didn't think much of either work. The stories were pedestrian and the novel's language didn't ring true, but I wasn't surprised because he didn't strike me as a writer. Always well turned out in a suit and tie, his trademark pipe clenched between his teeth when he wasn't using it to emphasise a point, he looked more like the businessman who had once hobnobbed with the powerful generals he was now fighting than the 'poor poet' he later claimed in his well-judged interviews with the foreign media. My prejudices weren't helped when he said that he was planning to publish five books in one year and fifty altogether before laying down his pen, as though literature was to be measured by the yard, but he wasn't perturbed when I turned him down. He just smiled as though I didn't understand and perhaps he was right. Within a few years, he was to emerge as the patron saint of the global environmental movement following his 'judicial murder' (the term used by John Major, the then British prime minister), by which time any number of London publishing houses were interested in his manuscripts, even commissioning his eldest son to write a memoir, aptly titled *In the Shadow of a Saint*.

I saw him again at a conference of African writers in Potsdam in the former East Germany in 1992 which I helped organise in my job on the Africa desk of the London-based *Index on Censorship* magazine. As soon as I arrived, the convener asked me if I knew one Ken Saro-Wiwa, who was in the country, had heard about the event and had invited himself over – at his own expense. I was irritated because I suspected he wouldn't fit in, but he was already on his way. True enough, he had hardly arrived when he admonished Biyi Bándélé for wearing 'torn jeans', much to everyone's amusement, especially when he added something about letting the side down, but he was also to prove the most entertaining. While the rest of us recited manifestoes to people just emerging from half a century of totalitarianism, he read from his collection of Ogoni folk tales. The story he chose had a refrain in his native Khana which he wrote on the blackboard and rehearsed with the audience beforehand so that the whole thing became a kind of sing-along. They loved it. They had braved a bleak mid-winter evening for a little African warmth and he was giving it to them, a broad grin on his face as he took them through the unfamiliar words. Afterwards, he said something about the plight of his people before doing a brisk trade with his hurriedly written books on the Ogoni question.

He and the cause had become one, indivisible, which explains why he needed to minimise the centrality of his Ijaw precursor, the enigmatic Major Isaac Adaka Boro, who had already identified the problems confronting the region and without whom no story about the Niger Delta – or Nigeria, same difference – will be complete but who seems to have been erased from whatever history books we are now writing.[9] Indeed, Saro-Wiwa said nothing that Boro hadn't said more succinctly before him. In Boro's autobiography, *The Twelve-Day Revolution*, he argued with the foresight that Saro-Wiwa was later to claim as one of his own compelling attributes that the Niger Delta had become the 'booty' of Nigeria by the mid-1960s and that, in consequence, the day was approaching when the indigenous people would have to take up arms and fight for their right to self-determination.[10] Like Saro-Wiwa after him, he was distressed by the dearth of amenities even as new oil wells were sunk and more and more pipes crisscrossed the farms and villages; unlike Saro-Wiwa, who eschewed

---

9 For instance, Boro is notably absent from Toyin Falola and Matthew M. Heaton's well regarded *A History of Nigeria*, Cambridge: Cambridge University Press, 2007.

10 Tony Tebekaemi, ed., *Major Isaac Adaka Boro: The Twelve-Day Revolution*, Benin City: Idodo Umeh Publishers, 1982.

violence, he openly took up arms against the state following his declaration of the Niger Delta Republic in 1966, which was about the same time Saro-Wiwa was unsuccessfully applying for a job from the same Shell which he nevertheless claimed he knew 'spelt wicked foreboding' as far back as 1958, when he was a scholarship student at the elite Government College Umuahia (and where he 'set a record which may be equalled, never beaten'). Boro and his volunteer force of 150 men were captured and sentenced to death, but the civil war broke out before he could be executed and he was drafted back into the army to fight the 'rebels' because, he judged, being under the Big Three was marginally better than being under just one of them. He was killed in action the following year, apparently shot in the back.

Boro was clearly a remarkable man, but Saro-Wiwa was having none of it. Significantly, Boro is mentioned in only one of many books, *On a Darkling Plain: An Account of the Nigerian Civil War* (1989), where he makes just three brief appearances, none of them illuminating. In the first, Saro-Wiwa quotes someone claiming that Boro's act of 'farcical recklessness' in waging war against the state was 'sinisterly bewildering to his people'; in the second, he writes that Boro's people were delighted at the news of his release so that he could wage another war (their sinister bewilderment notwithstanding); in the third, he claims that he was deeply touched when he heard of Boro's death and assured the delegation which called on him that the good work Boro had begun would live on after him. And that is all. No mention that Boro had also foreseen the importance of the environment long before the advent of Greenpeace by forbidding his men from indiscriminately killing animals or felling trees because, he said, harming nature harms us, who are also part of nature. Boro termed this the Law of Mutual Preservation.

No mention, either, that Boro only embarked on his act of 'farcical recklessness' in response to the first military coup of 15 January 1966, which he declared unconstitutional, saying he knew then that 'the day had dawned on the Niger Delta' and that, if nothing was done, 'we would throw ourselves into perpetual slavery'. One year later, during the civil war and with his conversion still a long way off, Saro-Wiwa himself accepted a post as civilian administrator for the port of Bonny in the newly created Rivers State; as he wrote to his eldest son, Junior, Nigeria had been good to him: 'I became a cabinet minister the year after I left University and the world was always at my feet. I did not even have to plan a future. Things happened to me.' By his own account, it was at this time that he formed his lifelong 'bond' with officers of the Third Marine Commando Battalion stationed in Port Harcourt, accounting for what he himself termed his 'indulgent attitude toward military rule in Nigeria'. Among those he was friendly with was his neighbour in the Government Reservation Area, the then Major Sani Abacha; by an irony of fate in a story replete with them, his other neighbour was Edward Kobani, one of the chiefs whose slaying he was to hang for.

For the converted, new-look Saro-Wiwa, the twin culprits of Ogoni's woes were the Federal Military Government of Nigeria and Shell Petroleum Development Company, the latter by far the biggest of the oil giants operating in the Niger Delta. The following incident gives a good idea of how the one colluded with the other in what Saro-Wiwa, echoing Boro, called 'the political marginalisation, economic strangulation, slavery and possible extinction of the Ogoni'. On 12 June 1993, the day of the election that Babangida was to annul two months later, an oil pipeline belonging to Shell began to leak near the village of Korokoro in Rivers

State. The community immediately reported the matter to Shell but heard nothing for three months, during which time oil flowed unabated into the creeks and farmlands around the village, damaging one of the most fragile eco-systems in the world. By September, with still no word from Shell, the community made fresh representations, calling on Shell to clear the sludge and pay adequate compensation. Another month passed and nothing happened, and then, on 25 October, a detachment of twenty-four military police laid siege to the village for five hours, killing and maiming and raping.

Thus the Task Force on Internal Security set up by the Rivers State Government, Order No. 4149, Restoration of Law and Order in Ogoniland. It was led by Major (later Lieutenant Colonel) Paul Okuntimo, whose orientation is best captured in his own words. The fact that he was being recorded at the time for broadcast on the state-owned Nigerian Television Authority is almost as salutary as what he actually said:

> The first three days . . . of operation, I operated in the night. Nobody knows where I was coming from. What I will just do I will just take some detachment of soldiers, they will just stay at four corners of the town. They . . . have automatic [rifles] that sold death. If you hear the sound you will freeze. And then I will equally now choose about 20 [soldiers] and five them . . . grenades . . . explosives . . . very hard one. So we shall surround the town at night. The machine gun with 500 rounds will open up. When 4 or 5 like that open up and then we are throwing grenades and they are making 'eekpuwaa'. What do you think people are going to do? And we have already put roadblock on the main road, we didn't want anybody to start running . . . so the option we made was that we shall drive all these

boys, all these people into the bush with nothing except their pant and the wrapper they are using that night.[11]

By mid-1994, Okuntimo's Task Force had overrun all 126 Ogoni villages, aided by the semi-automatic rifles, pump-action shotguns and tear gas that Shell later admitted paying for; but the government's failure to silence MOSOP, whose international profile was helped in great measure by the activities and public pronouncements of the Task Force itself, ensured the execution of its leadership following the killings of the chiefs on 21 May that same year.

All four of the chiefs slain that day were well known to Saro-Wiwa. One of them, Samuel N. Orage, an accountant, was the surrogate father of Saro-Wiwa's first wife, Maria; the pair met in his house, and Saro-Wiwa claimed he had such great love for Samuel N. Orage that he would never openly contradict him. The older brother, Theophilous B. Orage, he knew less well but nevertheless considered him family. The third chief, Albert Badey, was a former commissioner in Rivers State whom he had known since childhood; but it was Edward Kobani, his elder by six years, whom he knew best, having stayed with him and his wife, 'the beautiful and gentle Rose', in their house in Port Harcourt during the long university vacations, an act of kindness he claimed he would never forget even after he and Kobani fell out.

Nobody knows exactly what happened on that bloody Saturday because no proper police investigation was conducted and no forensic evidence was offered at the subsequent tribunal. The proceedings themselves were 'a travesty of law and justice', the title of a subsequent report

---

11 'The Ogoni Crisis: A Case-Study of Military Repression in Southeastern Nigeria', *Human Rights Watch*, Vol. 7, No. 5, July 1995.

undertaken on behalf of the Law Society of England and Wales. Even getting an audience with the prisoners at the military camp they were held in was a problem; for instance, supporters had difficulty seeing Dr Ledum Mitee, deputy president of MOSOP (and the only one to be acquitted):

On 26 June, 1994 three people went to see the Minister at Bori Military Camp. They were Oronto Douglas and Uche Onyeagocha, both Nigerian lawyers, and Nicholas Ashton-Jones, a British representative of the environmental group, Pro Natura. Douglas subsequently published a report in the magazine, *Liberty*. On arrival at Bori, soldiers and a mobile policeman allowed them to see Mitee. Lieutenant Colonel Paul Okuntimo then arrived, drew his pistol and berated the security men for allowing the visitors in. He kicked the policeman and had him put into a cell. On Okuntimo's order the three visitors and their driver were flogged. Then Okintumo drove them away in a jeep. He said that he had ordered that Saro-Wiwa be taken to an unknown place, chained and denied food; that Saro-Wiwa and Mitee 'would never see the light'; that he and his men had risked their lives to protect Shell installations; that he would 'sanitize' Ogoniland and that the visitors were lucky not to have got themselves killed. His first reaction had been to shoot their legs. The three visitors and their driver were detained until the morning of 29 June.

On 23 March 1995 I met one Mr. Onyeagocha. He told me that he had been detained for four days and given 100 lashes for trying to see the defendants. At that stage, I had not seen Mr. Douglas's article. Hence I did not discuss the details of the incident with him. On my return to England I wrote to Mr. Ashton-Jones enclosing a copy of the *Liberty* article and asking if it was correct. Mr. Ashton-Jones replied on 8 April . . . It will be seen that he agrees with the account given by Mr. Douglas but makes the point that he was flogged 'less severely than the others'.[12]

According to the unremittingly antagonistic prosecution witnesses, it seems that the chiefs were holding a meeting in the palace of His Royal Highness, Chief James Bagia, the Gbenemene of Gokana, when one of the commercial motorcycles popularly known as okadas pulled up some-time before noon and its driver said that Saro-Wiwa had told his followers that the people at the meeting 'were sharing money given to them by Government and Shell,' and that 'they [the youths] should come to the venue of the meeting to deal with you [the chiefs]'. A few minutes later, the palace was invaded by a mob of up to two thousand, some on okadas, three or four to a machine, others on foot armed with clubs, machetes, bottles, iron rods, broken blocks, stones and a garden rake. The leader of the mob shouted 'E-sho-be' to applause and directed that they kill one Celestine Meabe, who was set upon and 'the whole crowd impounded around me and beat me to a state of complete coma'. Meabe survived to become one of the chief prosecution witnesses.

A second witness, Alhaji Mohammed Kobani, younger brother of Chief Edward Kobani and the main source concerning the events of that day, said that he was attacked but was rescued and taken into a room in the palace, where he was able to shield his brother. Someone outside then directed the mob to go and bring the chiefs. Four of them were marched out, including Chief Albert Badey and the Orage brothers. They were set upon. They managed to stagger back into the palace but were attacked again as

---

12 Ibid., 184–5.

they huddled in a corner. Chief Badey made a bid to escape and was pursued; Chief Samuel N. Orage was beaten to death 'on the spot'. Chief Edward Kobani and Chief Theophilous B. Orage, whose right eye had been pierced in the first attack outside, were stripped nearly naked and the latter was led out of the palace. Alhaji Kobani said that his brother, whom he tried to help, was sliced on his back and hands with a broken bottle by one of the assailants while another buried the teeth of the garden rake in his skull. A third shoved a pole up his anus. Later, somebody was heard to say, 'Rise up now and go and contest the election with Ken Saro-Wiwa.'

Seeing that his brother was dead, Alhaji Kobani fled to the shrine behind the palace because, as he later told a British journalist, 'I am an Ogoni man and I know churches are just window dressing.' He said that if he had entered a church or a mosque 'they would have killed me there' but that their 'fetish belief' made them afraid that the repercussions 'would be on their families for generations'. However, he was helped in no small part by the courage of the Gbenemene, who hurried from his sick daughter's bedside when he heard 'crying and wailing of people around me' and refused the mob's demand that he make a libation for attack. He made a libation for peace instead and then entered the shrine to await help. That was about 2 p.m. Unknown to them, soldiers at a nearby checkpoint, as well as police in Bori, the main Ogoni town, refused to leave their posts when they were told what was going on because, they said, there was no senior officer around to order them to do so.

Chief Badey, meanwhile, who was last seen fleeing the palace, almost made it to a waiting taxi in the company of another intended victim, Chief Francis S. Kpai, but the mob proved too much for them. They then headed to the

Methodist Church but found that way also blocked. A woman offered them shelter and locked them in an inner room but gave them up after being threatened. A sympathiser then apparently helped Chief Badey to a bench, but the mob circled around him saying that they were going to kill him and then proceeded to beat him to death with 'all types of things such as bottles, stones, sticks, blocks and any other things they can lay their hands on'. Chief Kpai fared better. According to his own testimony, he was beaten, stripped and dragged back to the palace, where he was left for dead. When he came to, he saw Chief Kobani being beaten as his brother tried to rescue him. He then followed Alhaji Kobani into the shrine and confirmed that the Gbemenene made a libation for peace but added that some members of the mob fetched fuel to torch the shrine until one of their number prevailed upon them to desist.

As some of the mob assailed the shrine, others commandeered a white VW Beetle. Two witnesses on their way back from a fishing expedition said that they saw a large group of people pushing the car and were made to kneel down and swear never to reveal what they had seen. One of the witnesses said that he saw the naked corpse of a fat man inside the car and the corpses of two others being carried on an 'improvised stretcher', one of which he identified as that of Chief Theophilous B. Orage, the only victim whose killing was apparently not witnessed by anybody. The car was then set alight. Meanwhile, Chief Theophilous B. Orage's daughter, who was staying in the family compound two-and-a-half kilometres away, was informed by a breathless okada driver that 'they have beaten your father [and] you need to rescue him'. She hurried over but was unable to gain access to the palace for the crowd. She noticed a car burning in the distance. Someone who recognised her advised her to leave. She was set upon but managed to reach the okada; as she sped off, she heard someone shout, 'Slit her throat!' The scanty police report the following day observed that the car was pushed into the thick bush and that portions of flesh suspected to be the remains of the murdered chiefs were found at the scene. A relative of the Orage brothers later claimed that 'some parts of their bodies were eaten'.

The killings were the excuse for the soon-to-be-promoted Major Okuntimo to up his productivity rate. Exactly one month afterwards, he boasted to three activists that he was going to sanitise Ogoniland and that MOSOP 'would be history' by the time he was finished. The activists, who were detained and flogged for clustering around the military detention camp Saro-Wiwa was held in, also said that the major talked at length about how much he was doing for both Shell and the government. He even complained that he had almost got himself killed during one of his operations, which was why he had ordered that Saro-Wiwa be chained hand and leg for sixty-five consecutive days and deprived of food, although he denied this during a meeting a few months later in the presence of Saro-Wiwa himself and his leading counsel, Chief Gani Fáwęhinmi. Later, after it was all over, after Saro-Wiwa was dead and General Abacha was also dead and we were supposed to be enjoying the dividends of democracy, Okuntimo told the Human Rights Violations Investigations Commission that was supposed to be proof of our democracy that he was in fact the Messiah of the Ogoni people, only they didn't know it: 'If God did not send me [to] Ogoniland, there would be no Ogonis today. I was a saviour, not a butcher. I am their redeemer. I am the embodiment of truth. You people should be grateful to me that you are living. You should worship me.'

General Abacha's determination to find Saro-Wiwa guilty was demonstrated the day after the killings when the

military administrator of Rivers State, Lieutenant Colonel
Dauda Komo, addressed a lengthy press conference in which
he blamed the murders on the 'reckless and irresponsible
terror group of the MOSOP element', and called Saro-
Wiwa a 'dictator who has no accommodation and no room
for any dissenting view'. Saro-Wiwa was immediately
taken into custody and charged before the Ogoni Civil
Disturbances Special Tribunal with procuring and counsel-
ling six men to kill the chiefs, but the case was a mess and
the government knew it, which was why the tribunal had
to reinvent the law of murder in order to achieve its verdict.
The proceedings of the trial itself were a farce. The chair,
Justice Ibrahim Auta, who said that the case was one of
'simple murder' before any evidence had been given, openly
admitted at the start that, 'I am directly answerable to the
Commander-in-Chief, I am not answerable to any other
person,' and he refused to record any evidence that
favoured the accused, on the grounds that the tribunal
'records only what it considers necessary' (hence Saro-
Wiwa's quip about only seeing kangaroos on the bench).
The defence counsel, who were harassed, beaten and even
detained by the soldiers guarding the premises, and who
were continually hectored by Justice Auta as 'a pack of
noisemakers who impose themselves on clients', 'human
rights abusers' and 'an irresponsible lot', were eventually
forced to withdraw when the tribunal refused to admit a
videotape in evidence on the grounds that it may have been
tampered with.

The tape, which was in fact being used by Nigerian missions abroad as part of the government's inept propaganda
campaign, would have proved that the chief prosecution
witness, Alhaji Mohammed Kobani, was not averse to
changing his story to suit the occasion. In his original statement the day after the killings, he identified Paul Levura,

described as tall, slim and black, as the person who entered the palace at the height of the mayhem and offered to take Chief Theophilous B. Orage to safety. Almost a year later, when he was giving evidence, he changed his mind and said that it wasn't Levura after all but Nordu Eawo, who was described as short, stout and yellow. He did this in order to corroborate the testimony of Celestine Meabe, who had miraculously survived the attack at the palace but had failed to mention Eawo in his earlier statement. Both were convicted anyway, Levura because he couldn't give a satis-factory account of himself on the day in question, Eawo because he was 'a liar'. A third, Felix Nuate, was identified by Alhaji Kobani at a petrol station a full six months after the killings; yet the man he had earlier named as the person who wielded the garden rake was in police custody throughout the trial but never charged. Whether the detained man was eventually released depended on the vicissitudes of the Nigerian criminal justice system: during his first detention, Saro-Wiwa came across a young Ogoni boy who had spent over three years in prison because there was no one to sign a bail bond of ₦5000 (US$60) on his behalf.

More absurdly still, three of the convicted men, includ-ing Saro-Wiwa himself, were not even at the scene of the killings. John Kpunien was acknowledged by the tribunal to have been running errands elsewhere in Ogoniland but was convicted anyway on the grounds that 'the individual affected need not be physically present or directly person-ally participate in the act of civil disturbances' in order to be 'credited with the consequences' and be 'answerable for them'. The case against both him and Saro-Wiwa rested on a meeting they were alleged to have attended the previous year, during which Saro-Wiwa was supposed to have directed the youths to deal with thirteen named

'vultures' – including three of the murdered chiefs – for con-
spiring with the Federal Military Government and Shell to
destroy MOSOP. Kpunien said that he couldn't have been
at the meeting because he was on leave at the time and had
the documentation to prove it, but this was brushed aside
because, according to the tribunal's nightmare logic, 'Being
on leave does not exempt an individual from attendance at
meetings and failure to attend meetings does not exempt
the absent member from being bound by a decision of a
body organization of which he is a member.'

Saro-Wiwa, who was held to have 'wrongfully' organised
an election campaign rally which 'wrongfully' congregated
a large crowd of his 'fanatical' youths, thereby creating 'a
riotous situation' which led directly to the murders, denied
that any such meeting ever took place. The evidence is all
on his side because the two witnesses who claimed to have
attended the rally, Meabe and David Keenom, proved unre-
liable. Keenon contradicted himself on several points,
including his age, occupation and qualifications, and only
affirmed under cross-examination that Saro-Wiwa had
directed members of the newly formed youth league to
deal with the vultures, contrary to his earlier statement to
the police. Saro-Wiwa himself, who could be 'caustic and
brusque', according to Junior, counted both men among
the 'thugs, the dregs of Ogoni society'. These two in
particular, he wrote, 'belong to the lunatic fringe of the
Ogoni Movement' which they had sought to use 'for their
selfish purposes'. He was pleased they had been 'flushed . . .
out early' but regretted that the prosecution had 'lionised
these vermin, giving them an opportunity to display
their depravity before the world'. He rued the fact that
Keenon, in particular, was able to 'continue his life of
infamy, extorting money from Ogoni villagers' by threatening to incriminate them in the killings.

More damaging again to the case were allegations by two witnesses for the prosecution that they, along with Keenon, Meabe and four others, were forced to give false testimony in order to secure the convictions. One of them, Charles Danwi, a musician, said that he had been detained at Alhaji Kobani's house for some days, during which he was told: 'This is a military government that anything they want to do to me they can do it.' He said that he finally capitulated and made a statement but they rejected it 'and ask me to copy a statement already made by them'. In return, they promised him a house anywhere in the country, a contract from Shell and money to buy musical instruments with. He said that there was a follow-up meeting, also in Alhaji Kobani's house, where representatives from Shell, the Federal Military Government and members of the Kobani, Orage and Badey families wanted to ensure that he 'made a statement that will involve Ken and MOSOP officials so that they will kill them', and that Alhaji Kobani himself never knew any of those he identified. He added, finally, that members of the Kobani family roped in a Catholic priest, but that when he objected to using the Church as cover 'they quarrel with me'.

As Saro-Wiwa himself said at the time, 'My murder is being officially planned and executed,' but few suspected that it would be carried out so swiftly. The sentences were imposed on 31 October 1995. They were approved by the Provisional Ruling Council, the military in this case being both judge and final court of appeal, on 8 November. Two days later, the Ogoni Nine were hanged before noon at Port Harcourt prison. According to unconfirmed reports, Saro-Wiwa asked to see his wife. This was refused. Then he asked to see his ninety-one-year-old father to give him his pipe and wallet. This, too, was refused. Afterwards, the corpses were soaked in acid and buried in a secret location.

Assuming that General Abacha wanted to make a point, his timing was perfect. The Commonwealth heads of government were just then assembling in Auckland, New Zealand, for their bi-annual powwow, with Nigeria, only one of two member countries still under military rule, top of the agenda. A distraught President Nelson Mandela (who had apparently flown in overnight to plead on Saro-Wiwa's behalf) subsequently led the call for Nigeria's suspension, to which Abacha retorted, 'I do not blame Mandela because, having spent 27 years in detention, he has lost touch with the global socio-political trend.' Honourable ministers promptly followed suit, including Iyorwuese Hagher, the minister of state for power and steel, who argued at length in a newspaper article that Mandela's action had shown him to be the house nigger of 'the new slave masters', that is, the old slave masters, including 'the South African apartheid machinery'. Witness, for instance, how easily they had wrested him 'from the control of the black militancy of Winnie' in order that he might better 'perform the dance of the stooges'. Another minister, this time for agriculture, Professor Adémọ́lá Adéṣínà, went even further. 'How can somebody spend 27 years in prison and still be sane?' he queried, and then, working himself up to a state of hysteria, pronounced Mandela 'a white man in black skin and no white man likes the blacks'. Indeed: Mandela's own description of the regime as 'illegitimate, barbaric and arrogant' missed only stupid.

And then it turned out that it was all a dreadful misunderstanding; that Abacha hadn't meant anything derogatory in his reference to Mandela's long years of imprisonment; and that what actually happened was that, 'the statement . . . was not in fact his exact words', but that 'the wordings [sic] were amplifications by the press of what the head of state said when he met with traditional rulers and leaders

93

of thought'. This was from Abacha's chief press secretary, David Attah, indulging the national pastime, which is that it's always somebody else's fault in Nigeria, especially when the latest victim of the country's terminally irresponsible press also happens to be 'a mature, calculating and self-respecting statesman'.[13] Shell, responding to Greenpeace's accusation that the company had blood on its hands, had originally insisted on quiet diplomacy in the week preceding the executions on the grounds that those who knew Africa best, like Mandela, had recommended such a course, and that, in any case, protesting against the government might achieve the opposite of the intended result. Two days after the executions, and with Mandela threatening the company's future in South Africa, Shell issued a news release claiming that the situation in the Niger Delta was 'fraught and complex', and that simplifying and distorting the facts 'in the service of a campaign or cause', however well-intentioned, was unhelpful. In his valedictory speech eighteen months later, the Nigerian-born British managing director of Shell, Brian Anderson, declared himself confident that what happened on 10 November 1995 'could not have been influenced by any activity that I personally or Shell could have taken'.

Saro-Wiwa's younger brother, Dr Owens Wiwa, disagrees. He said that he first met Anderson in April 1995, when the trial was well underway, and begged him to convince the authorities to allow his brother the medical attention he was denied. Anderson said that he would see what he could do, and shortly afterwards Saro-Wiwa was admitted into a military hospital. At a subsequent meeting, Dr Wiwa said that he had asked Anderson to intervene to

---

13   Adewale Maja-Pearce, 'The murderers in our midst', *Index on Censorship*, Vol. 1, 1996, 58–9.

stop the trial 'so that negotiations can start between Shell and the Ogoni people', but that Anderson replied that this would only be possible if MOSOP issued a press release stating that there was no environmental degradation in the Niger Delta. When Dr Wiwa refused to issue the press release – on his brother's instructions – Anderson informed him that he would no longer be available for discussions and directed him to Nnaemeka Achebe, head of PR (and now His Royal Highness, the Obi of Onitsha).

For his part, Dr Wiwa said that Achebe stressed the importance of continuing dialogue but was never at the other end of the phone when he called. Achebe denied that Shell had ever demanded a press release denying environmental degradation when I interviewed him at the Shell headquarters overlooking the River Thames in London. He was promoted and stationed there after denying that he had told an American journalist in his 'plush Lagos office with sweeping views of the Gulf of Guinea' that dictatorships were good for business because they delivered a stable environment. Achebe further denied saying that 'now in Nigeria there is acceptance, peace and continuity', claiming that he had in fact said the opposite, which was that 'frequent changes of government had resulted in fundamental shifts in economic policy and had created an unstable environment', but this was difficult to follow since there hadn't been 'frequent changes of government' (if only!), and the unstable environment in Ogoniland that had forced his company to withdraw had been generated despite the activities of the task force. Still, one has to sympathise over Shell's predicament; as Anderson once remarked, in Nigeria 'the government is in the oil industry and the oil industry is in government.'[14]

---

14   John Jennings, 'Dangerous Liaisons', *Index on Censorship*, Vol. 4, 1997, 50.

The situation in Ogoniland worsened after the executions. According to Ledum Mitee, the exiled acting president of MOSOP, it was doubtful whether even the government knew of the activities of Okuntimo's successor, Major Obi Umahi, although the journalists who fought the longest and hardest of any institution in Nigeria against military rule knew better.[15] They included two Rivers State correspondents who were detained and flogged for writing that the task force had impounded 120 copies of Saro-Wiwa's books. In the major's own words: 'I wanted to deal with you ruthlessly since you've taken it upon yourselves to bring down the government.'

It was only after Abacha's death on 8 June 1988, apparently in the arms of two prostitutes specially flown in from India, that revelations emerged of hit squads – K-Squad, Strike Force, Special Squad – responsible for eliminating opponents. One high-profile victim was 'Pa' Alfred Rewane, an industrialist and one of the founding members of Awólọ́wọ̀'s Action Group in 1951. He was killed by a single bullet to his heart when five gunmen broke into his house in Lagos in the early hours of 6 October 1995. Two of them herded his family and servants into a downstairs room while the others went upstairs, where their intended victim was getting dressed with the help of his steward. The gunmen beat up the steward and shoved him under the bed before shooting Rewane. They took

---

15 'The Press – and let me seize this very opportunity to stress this – has been magnificent, really magnificent, heroic, and one of these days, when there's more pleasure, we are going to erect a statue. I'm going to personally see to this, that a statue for heroism of the press is erected at a prominent place in this country. We must never, ever forget.' Wọlé Ṣóyínká, *Guardian on Sunday*, 17 October 1998. We hope he will yet fulfil his promise!

two briefcases of papers but left behind a sizable amount of cash.

Two days later, the inspector general of police, Ibrahim Coomassie, constituted a high-powered panel to investigate the shooting. The following day, the Lagos State Police Command announced that the killers, who were professionals, had left no clues, but two days later said that they had 'inadvertently left a number of formidable clues . . . for the police to work on', including the make of the car they came in, and the command assured that the police would 'prove people wrong on this matter [and] shall prove to everyone that we are capable of tracking [down] criminals'.[16]

On 27 October, the police announced they had apprehended seven people: the gateman and driver of the deceased, a 'friend' of the gateman, a 'hotelier', two vulcanisers and a 'job-seeker'. On 16 December, reporters were invited to the Federal Investigation and Intelligence Bureau headquarters to watch their videotaped confessions. Two days later, Coomassie himself announced that the police had 'made a breakthrough':

> It is an inside work. It is not assassination as people suspect. One of the staff arranged it. He has been arrested and he is in custody. Five other suspects have been arrested. One other has been killed by police in another armed robbery operation during a confrontation with police.[17]

The suspects were arraigned in court on 3 January 1986, but the case was adjourned four times: because five other

---

16   Ebere Ahamihu, 'Fresh rumblings over Rewane's murder', *Guardian on Sunday*, 10 October 1998.
17   Ibid.

subjects still at large were yet to be apprehended, or because the case file was with the investigating police officer who wasn't in the courtroom just then, or because one of the suspects had or hadn't died – everyone agreed, at any rate, that he had been sick. The case then went into abeyance until the following January – that is, exactly one year after the start of legal proceedings – when Coomassie announced that all the suspects had escaped from detention even as he disowned responsibility: 'Once a case is before a legally constituted court and the court, after hearing, pronounces judgement or remands them in prison custody, the police automatically hands off the case.'[18]

The revelations of official complicity in the assassination of Rewane came from no less a figure than Major Hamza Al-Mustapha, 'Abacha's Himmler'. He was arrested in October 1998, along with more than twenty other 'Abacha boys', including Ismaila Gwarzo, national security adviser; Brigadier-General Ibrahim Sabo, head of the Directorate of Military Intelligence; and Colonel Frank Omenka, former head of security at DMI. Under interrogation, Mustapha confessed that 'Abacha gave us license to kill'.[19] He said that Omenka was responsible for giving orders, and that he, Mustapha, was responsible for co-ordinating the assassinations with the DMI and military police. He said that the decision to murder Rewane was taken at a meeting in Abuja with Omenka, Gwarzo and Sabo, where it was agreed that the attack should be made to look like an armed robbery. Some 'miscreants' could be paraded before the public and then spirited out of the country. Rewane had been chosen because he was publicly funding the exiled National Democratic Coalition, the foreign-based umbrella group agitating

---

18   Ibid.
19   'Mustapha's Confessions', *Tell*, 21 December 1998.

for the actualisation of the annulled election, and because he was buying space in the press calling for the simultaneous restructuring of the country and the armed forces.

The other prominent victim was Alhaja Kudirat Abíọ́lá, the most vocal of the imprisoned chief's wives, who was shot dead in her car in the early morning of 4 June 1996 at a busy junction not far from the governor's lodge. According to Mustapha, it was Abacha himself who gave the order because, he said, one of the twenty-seven marabous he surrounded himself with told him to do so, the same marabous who also reputedly searched out one thousand newborn mice, padlocked their mouths with specially designed miniature padlocks and drowned them before their eyes opened, thus rendering Nigerians blind and mute. Others say it was because she had the ear of the diplomatic community at a time when Nigeria was spending significant sums on 'image-laundering' exercises, but her fate could have easily been sealed by the frequent – and abrasive – interviews this Yorùbá woman gave the BBC Hausa Service in perfect Hausa; radio, then and now, being by far the most important (even only) means of communication in large swathes of the North, where the predominantly farming population is in many ways even more marginalised than its southern counterparts.

Mustapha's confessions were repeated by Omenka, who bemoaned that 'the blood of Kudirat, Rewane and so many unknown others is on our heads' because they had been given 'the power to maim and kill if necessary', although he disclaimed final responsibility: 'Though Mustafa was my junior in rank, he occupied a more powerful position. He was [Abacha's] voice. The consequence of refusal was better imagined than experienced.'[20] In other words, the

---

20   *Tell*, 11 January 1999.

chain of command associated with a disciplined army had collapsed, so deeply had politics corrupted an institution which saw a general cower before a major. The only one who didn't spill the beans was Gwarzo, who Mustapha claims had convinced Abacha to kill Anthony Enahoro and Wọlé Ṣóyínká, the two most prominent exiles, by hiring hit men from Latin America and the Middle East. And then Abacha himself went and died (his marabous notwithstanding).

General Abdulsalami Abubakar, Abacha's third-in-command, assumed power on 9 June 1998 (his second-in-command, Lieutenant General Ọládipọ̀ Diya, had been sentenced to death for coup plotting but was released following Abacha's demise). In July, Abubakar announced his own programme for transition to civil rule to culminate on 29 May the following year, making it the shortest of all such programmes attempted since the military's second coming on New Year's Eve, 1984. To that end, he inaugurated yet another 'independent' electoral commission, the fourth such since the military began transferring power to the civilians in the 1970s. Given what they had been through, many Nigerians were sceptical, including General Àláni Akínrìnádé, a former chief of defence staff (1979–80) but now a retired opposition spokesperson:

> Have we forgotten how quickly that Abubakar played prominent roles in Babangida's and Abacha's administrations ... He cannot escape a fair share of the responsibility in creating Abacha's terror machine, details of whose atrocities are now being graphically revealed. He is keeping all those apparatuses intact. All the obnoxious decrees that were used to sustain Abacha's gulag are still in Abubakar's books and we hear that Gwarzo is detained under Decree 2. The

Army, Police, state security . . . which had been responsible
for the murder of several pro-democracy activists are kept
intact.[21]

Indeed, it was for this reason that the National Democratic Coalition called for a sovereign national conference
to 'undertake an appropriate restructuring of the Nigerian
polity as a means of establishing true federalism and political stability'. The two specific areas to be looked at were
power sharing on the one hand, and revenue generation
and allocation on the other, although it would also look at
'all other matters vital to the future progress, peaceful
co-existence and justice and harmony within the nation'.
This tallied with most southern opinion, including, above
all, the restive minorities in the Niger Delta, who declared
themselves no longer willing to accept 'our enslavement
in the fraudulent contraption called Nigeria' at the Ijaw
Youth Conference held at Kaiama, Bayelsa State on 11
December 1998.

The conference reached the conclusion any such conference was bound to reach, that the present arrangement was
intolerable, and it issued what it called the Kaiama Declaration, which rejected the so-called derivation principle
allowing communities only 3 percent of their resources
(down from 100 percent in 1953, 45 percent in 1970 and
20 percent in 1975) in favour of self-governance within 'a
federation of nationalities'. It also demanded 'the immediate withdrawal from Ijawland of all military forces of
occupation and repression by the Nigerian State' before
the end of the year, and the complete cessation of 'all exploration and exploration activities' by the oil companies,

---

21   Alani Akinrinade, 'Transition? What transition?', *Guardian*, 15
December 1998.

who were to desist from employing 'the services of the armed forces of the Nigerian State to "protect" its operations' lest they be regarded as 'an enemy'. Predictably, the 'armed forces of the Nigerian state' were deployed even before the ultimatum expired, when soldiers opened fire on a peaceful demonstration on 30 December. The demonstrators, who merely wanted to present a petition to the state military administrator, had been previously cleared by the state police commissioner, who ordered his men not to harm them. Twelve others were arrested and taken to the same Bori military camp where Saro-Wiwa had been held. Four days later, the death toll had risen to twenty-six as the military set up fifteen roadblocks on a seventeen-kilometre stretch of road; in the words of the military administrator: 'various groups . . . threatened the basic existence of the Federal Republic of Nigeria . . . in particular the Kaiama Declaration . . . which purportedly resolved to control all natural resources of Niger Delta and threats of war.'

The sentiments contained in the Kaiama Declaration were repeated at a conference held in Lagos. The keynote speech was given by Anthony Enahoro, the 'renowned' nationalist who first moved the motion for Nigeria's independence in 1953, who begged to oppose the declaration of a state of emergency in the 1962 Western Region because you never know where it might end and who now, in old age, had been harried into exile by Abacha because he still couldn't stay silent in the face of tyranny. In his address, he simply asked why the Abubakar administration ruled out a sovereign national conference in favour of a speedy transition programme unless it was afraid of the 'democratic decision-making process'. The question went to the heart of the unease. Most people at the time did believe that Abubakar would step down come 29 May 1999 because even the military understood that the bloody civilians were bloody well tired of them. At the same time, few believed that the military had any intention of handing over power to a government which might probe them, which was why they also included an act in the constitution they were preparing which forbade the constitution itself from doing so. Given the vast sums that were bandied about, the country's entire external debt could have been covered by a handful of generals and their cronies, hence the restriction on party registration; and hence, also, the emergence of the retired General Olúṣẹ́gun Ọbásanjọ́ as the leading presidential candidate of the People's Democratic Party (PDP) that was to sweep the elections.[22]

The first question was why the parties had to be registered at all; why they couldn't come together as free associations and take their chances at the polls. According to the rules, only parties with functioning offices in at least twenty-four of the thirty-six states and the Federal Capital Territory, Abuja, where they were to have their headquarters, could be provisionally registered to contest the forthcoming local government election. Nine out of twenty-four made it over this hurdle, but full registration depended on scoring a minimum of 5 percent of all votes in said twenty-four states and Abuja. The demand that parties

---

22   The first of these came in newspaper reports in early November 1998 when Chief Anthony Oni, Abacha's long-serving finance minister, said that Gwarzo had withdrawn US$1,331bn from the Central Bank of Nigeria in the last eighteen months of Abacha's rule at the insistence of the dictator himself. Later in the month, we were told that almost US$1bn in cash in different denominations had been 'recovered' from the Abacha family: US$625,263,187.19; £675,306, 884.93; and ₦252mn, all of it amounting to the annual budgets of thirty-three states. A further US$2bn was discovered to have been 'shared by two former ministers and a member of the Abacha family', according to Mallam Mohammed Haruna, chief press secretary to Abubakar.

have national spread was not in itself new or even particularly controversial. It had been a requirement in 1979 and was behind Babangida's justification for registering just two parties. The ostensible idea was to promote national unity – or, at least, discourage narrowly based ethnic politics – in such a diverse nation; the reality has been effectively to disenfranchise the minorities who between them amount to one-third of the population, as well as ensure the self-succession of the cabal in power.

In fact, this cabal had been handing over to itself since 1 October 1960, hence the recent passing of the baton from President Buhari (he of the murderous retroactive decree) to President Tinúbú. As for 1999, Ọbásanjọ́ was a perfect fit to swap khaki for agbádá in order to maintain northern hegemony under the guise of power shift. Ọbásanjọ́, who couldn't bear criticism of the institution which served him well, went on record more than once to say that the military shouldn't be disgraced out of power. He also happened to be a southerner, a Yorùbá, from the same town – Abẹ̀òkúta – as the Abíọ́lá whose mandate he was quick to renounce on the grounds that he wasn't the messiah Nigerians were looking for. More importantly, he proved himself a safe pair of hands when called upon to perform a similar duty two decades earlier (even putting General Murtala Muhammed on the ₦20 note), and he'd proved he could be counted on to do the same again, which was precisely why he was so disliked by his own people, who voted against him even in his own constituency.

But the objection to Ọbásanjọ́, to whose campaign Babangida was rumoured to have donated US$50mn, went beyond the merely personal, beyond the fact, say, that he caused soldiers to burn down the house of a man who sang rude things about the military that was now – on

Ọbásanjọ́'s orders – doing the very thing that had brought them into disrepute. The problem went deeper than the man who handed over power to an elected civilian administration and who would now propose, two troubled decades later, to effectively hand over power to himself. In the process, a 'democratic' Ọbásanjọ́ administration would establish the precedent of military rule by other means – 'army arrangeement', as Fẹlá put it – in a country with precious few precedents in such a short history. Chief Olú Fálaè, Ọbásanjọ́'s adversary who never stood a chance, was not a hemp-dazed musician with an outrageous life-style but a former secretary to the federal government under Babangida, a presidential aspirant in 1983 and now hoping to realise his ambition, put it this way: 'The ongoing transition is aimed at transforming the military out of uniform to perpetual leadership of the country ... The whole exercise is fashioned out of Abdul Nasser of Egypt with the ultimate aim of ensuring that the military retains its political power ... The military has no more to offer the people of this country, whether in or out of uniform.'[23]

On the other hand, Fálaè's campaign scarcely inspired confidence, as I discovered when I tried to join him in the week leading up to the presidential election:

> He promised me a place on his 16-seater aircraft when I saw him at his party headquarters in Lagos, but when I arrived in Abuja, the centre of operations, I spent two frustrating days being pushed and shoved by assorted hangers-on who clearly weren't going to let 'Mr President' out of their sight. The first day I never even made it up the steps. I got into the aircraft on the second day, having been reassured by Mr President that this time I was definitely among the chosen,

23 *Punch*, 17 December 1998.

only to be confronted by two elderly men – northerners both – squabbling over who was senior and therefore entitled to the one remaining seat. It was clearly beyond the powers of Mr President to call them to order, although he did mutter something about hiring a second aircraft but this, too, turned out to be beyond him. There were no other journalists in his entourage: they were all with Obasanjo, who was treating them well, judging by the column inches devoted to him – and this was a man who once put up a notice at the entrance to his farm banning journalists, along with women and dogs.[24]

The elections were designed from the start to produce a preordained outcome. We have a good idea of what transpired because a coalition of civil society organisations came together as the Transitional Monitoring Group, courtesy of foreign funding, so concerned was the international community – that is, the 'West' – that Nigeria join the post–Cold War democratic fold. About 8,000 observers were fielded throughout the thirty-six states and Abuja to monitor the national and presidential elections. Each observer was given a questionnaire seeking the following: whether the presiding officer had all the materials; whether parties' agents were present; whether accreditation began at 8 a.m. and polling at 11 a.m.; whether there was added security; whether anyone interfered with the voting process and if so, how; and whether polling closed at 2:30 p.m. There was space at the end for the results and for any additional comments arising out of any misconduct the observers may have witnessed.

These additional comments, which were made by about a quarter of the observers, are the more interesting part of

---

24   Maja-Pearce, 'Army Arrangement'.

the exercise for anyone but a psephologist. Such was the 'demonstration of craze' that one observer of the national assembly election in Igbo-Eze North local government area (LGA) of Enugu State was moved to lament: 'What an unbridled show of political gangsterism. What a disconsolate loss of the electoral mandate. What an abomination, an abuse of trust, and a pseudo-political presentation. What a heinous ambushade of the transition to civil rule programme.'[25] The following week, another observer at the same LGA was forced to flee when 'the party thugs got together probably for a plot violent' when he refused to condone 'their mode of election', even turning down 'a gift of money'. Less fortunate was an observer in Anambra State who was 'beaten mercilessly . . . as the presiding officer and the poll clerk go on thumb printing and at the same time voting'.

Violence was the dominant feature of the election in all the states in the South-east and south-south, which was where PDP clinched victory. Of these, the worst affected were the core oil-producing states. In Uyo, the capital of Akwa Ibom, the leader of the TMG was beaten and held hostage for five hours while 'a group of students . . . went around the area and collected boxes from other stations and finally destroyed and burnt 5 boxes because they claimed they were not paid by the parties'. In Kolokuma/Okopuma LGA in Bayelsa, Egbesu were everywhere intimidating the few citizens who turned up to vote: 'I . . . got a report from a police inspector that some boys came and rounded them up that they are the Egbesu boys with guns and if they don't go away from [there] they would kill all

---

25 Adewale Maja-Pearce, *1999 Annual Report*, Lagos: Civil Liberties Organisation, 2001, 2. Unless otherwise indicated, subsequent quotes in this chapter can be found here.

of them.'[26] In Sagbama LGA of the same state, a certain Inspector D_ U_ was busy in a number of polling stations ensuring that the TMG was 'deprived from observing' while groups of boys with 'long matchets [machetes] hidden in their seam trousers' went about 'intimidating eligible voters'. In Gokana LGA in Rivers, the home of the late Ken Saro-Wiwa, 'there was complete violence [sic] disorder'.

Although PDP was the most visible in rigging, here as elsewhere in the country, all the parties participated, most notoriously the All People's Party (dubbed Abacha People's Party on account of the number of his former cronies in its ranks), which initially claimed that the PDP paid ₦2.5mn to each of the thirty-seven electoral commission offices in the country, and ₦2mn to each state police force. Shortly afterwards, the party's national chair demanded that its members 'outrig' the opposition. 'Don't tell me tomorrow that somebody had rigged the election and that's why you did not win,' he said at a pre-election rally in Enugu. 'No, this is not an excuse. We have heard that 101 times. You should rig; all we want is to win the elections at all costs.'

---

26 'Currently, Egbesu is known as a spiritual instrument of warfare that vaccinates Ijaw fighters against bullets. Since the 1990s, Ijaw youths from the Niger Delta region of Nigeria have been engaged in inter-ethnic as well as oil-related conflict with the federal government. Reporting on data collected from participant observation and interviews with relevant authorities, we present Egbesu as a "just war" philosophy, a set of war ethics delineating the criteria for a just cause of war (*jus ad bellum*), just conduct during war (*jus in bello*) and just actions after war (*jus post bellum*), that also establishes a reward system through the promise of victory for just warriors. The promise of victory seems to be the essence of the conception of Egbesu as a spiritual instrument for victory in warfare, translated into immunity to bullets and other enemy weapons.' Elias Courson and Michael E. Odijie, 'Egbesu: An African Just War Philosophy and Practice', *Journal of African Cultural Studies*, 3 February 2020.

The PDP, for its part, rubbished the 'lamentations' of 'con-genital failures' and 'distressed political widows' intent on 'trying to derail the transition by beginning these cock-and-bull stories of yester-years'.[27]

One clue to the rigging was the number of returns filled in by the same hand, showing collusion on the part of some of the observers. In the national assembly election, for instance, more than half the returns in seven of the thirteen LGAs in Èkìtì, three of the seventeen in Ògún and ten of the fifteen in Oǹdó – all in the South-west – were filled in by the same hand and all for Alliance for Democracy, the third registered party representing that region. Another clue was the claims of high voter turnout in elections char-acterised by widespread apathy. Ishielu LGA in Ebonyi, for example, recorded 100 percent turnout in twenty-seven of the thirty polling stations monitored in the national assem-bly election. Isin LGA in Kwara recorded 100 percent turnout in fourteen of the twenty polling stations moni-tored in the presidential election and yet even the observer commented that 'people did not really turn-out [sic]'. In some states in the south-south, the figures were out of this world. For instance, in the national assembly election in Bayelsa, where a number of polling stations in all eight LGAs recorded 100 percent turnout, one station in Brass LGA recorded 10,500 voters, all of whom voted for PDP. Out of the thirty polling stations monitored, thirteen gave no results and all the rest bar three went to PDP, all but one of them with 100 percent of the vote.

Low voter turnout was reported by an overwhelming number of observers, as witness the following nationwide selection for the national assembly election: Ganye LGA, Adamawa: 'The turn up of voters to the poll was very poor.

---

27   Maja-Pearce, 'Army Arrangement'.

Saturday being the Ganye market day everybody was very busy buying and selling at the market instead of going out to exercise their civil rights'; Damban LGA in Bauchi: 'The turn out of voters was very very poor out of the six hundred registered voters . . . only 34 came for accreditation out of the 34 only 29 came to cast their votes. The turn out of women was very low only three women came out for accreditation'; Nkanu East LGA, Enugu: 'Turn out was generally poor and people evidently showed lack of interest in the process'; Gombe LGA in Gombe: '70% of the voters did not come out for accreditation.'

Additionally, the Islamic culture in some parts of the North prevented women from voting because 'men could not allow their wives to remain in such an open public place of polling station'. In this same polling station in Wammako LGA in Sokoto, 'there was also a problem in inking the voter's left thumb nail' because there was no female official to undertake the task and 'the culture of the area does not allow an adult male to touch a married female voter'. In an ironic reversal, at another polling station in the same state women were sent by their husbands to vote for them 'but the presiding officer noticed it that they were sent forcefully to vote but refused to [allow] them according to the rules and regulations of the election'. In four polling stations in Dutse LGA in Jigawa, women comprised just 36 of the 790 voters. In Zaria LGA in Kaduna, 'married women don't normally come to the polling station [and] are usually represented by their husbands or their representatives'. In Kumbutso LGA in Kano, 'only seven (7) women showed up for accreditation and polling'. In Birnin-Kebbi LGA in Kebbi, 'the people of the area . . . has a kind of tradition of voting for their wives, depending on the agreement reached [between] the agents of all the parties'. In Gusau LGA in Zamfara, 'no single woman came for voting'.

However, some other, non-Islamic cultures appeared to find the presence of women exercising their fundamental human right equally distasteful. In a tragic incident in Akwa-Ibom,

> an unconfirmed report from Eket Ward 111 had it that a prospective female voter met her untimely death when a male voter pushed her out of the voting queue on the excuse that women were not supposed to come out for voting. The female voter fell down and died instantly as a result of that incident.

By contrast, women voters in Plateau in the Middle Belt sometimes outnumbered men. In one polling station in Bokkos LGA, 108 women voted as against 62 men; in Langbang LGA the ratio was 215 to 196; in Pankshin LGA, 159 to 140. Additionally, one observer in Kòṣòfé LGA in Lagos State found that 'the number of women who were present are more than those of the men'. This was attributed to the fact that 'nowadays women are more interested in the political affairs than ever before'.

The TMG returns identified a number of reasons for the low turnout. Babangida's annulment of the 12 June 1993 presidential election and Abacha's tortured five-year transition programme had made the electorate cynical; as one observer in Etche LGA in Rivers wrote:

> There was loss of interest and apathy due to voter fatigue and loss of confidence among the electorates. The elders especially were not seen. So also were women. Those I talked to expressed misgivings in the whole exercise. They believe that the Nigerian electoral process is fraught with malpractice and it is a waste of time to go out voting.

Staying away was an opportunity 'to show their cumulative frustrations', according to an observer in Darakin Tofa LGA in Kano. Besides, there was a general feeling that the outcome had already been decided. In Kaduna North LGA in Kaduna, 'Many of the voters who came around to vote saying it has [been] arranged that Obasanjo is going to emerge winner so there is no need for them to cast their vote'; in Ajeromi-Ifelodun LGA in Lagos, 'they believe that government was behind a particular party and the need to vote has been defeated'. This view was confirmed by PDP agents themselves, who shouted at an observer in Isuikwuato LGA in Abia who refused to be bribed 'that I should go to blazes that the man that will be chosen president has already been chosen, that I'm just there wasting my time observing what I did not know'; and they added: 'The worst of it was when he threaten [sic] my life & my family, saying that he knows my family so well & that I should mind what I do here because they will seriously deal with me.'

Low voter turnout made it easier to rig the election, with or without – but usually with – the connivance of the electoral commission. Children were especially favoured, presumably because they were cheaper. In Maiduguri LGA in Borno: 'From my estimation nothing less than 40 percent of the voters were underaged'; in Esan South East LGA in Edo: 'The Party agent and the presiding officer allowed the underaged to vote'; in Zaria LGA in Kaduna: 'Accreditation of underaged was observed'; in Langtang South LGA in Plateau: 'I observed that some of the people that came for the voting are under aged children.' Also used were students in nearby tertiary institutions. In Uyo LGA in Akwa Ibom, 'a group of students moved into the polling station, forced the parties' agents out and forced the presiding officer to stamp and sign the ballot papers'. In Ihitue/Uboma LGA in Imo:

I saw some of my fellow students whom I interviewed and learnt that they were paid N500, some N300 to come and vote for a particular party (PDP) mostly for the Senatorial election in which Nwajuba was the contestant. They told me that up to 40 percent of them were transported to come to the voting in my place alone.

Even villagers were paid to vote, as one witness from Ningi LGA in Bauchi observed:

The whole exercise which was supposed to commence by 8 o'clock simultaneously did not go as planned, some started as early as 7:30 a.m. A polling station I was passing along my way to Nasaru polling station called 'maternity' was accrediting its voters as at then, meanwhile a look at the polling box revealed as at that time that half of it was filled up with ballot papers. There was no sign of any security agent there. On reaching the intended Nasaru polling station, I met an inspector and a sergeant. Then it was 8 a.m. when the accreditation exercise commenced. However, instead of asking all that was accredited to wait till the voting time, each was allowed to go, not heading to a particular direction, on throwing a glance some metres away I saw another polling station that was where these people were going. When I curiously pay attention, I discovered that they were being accredited there too.

When the voting time was due, the police inspector left for an unknown destination, as people started voting, there was no queue and the voters were given more than one ballot paper to thumb-print in favour of PDP, yet the sergeant couldn't utter a word, and there wasn't an APP agent around to protest either. From there, the same people will go to the nearby polling station (which is also at vicinity) and do the same. It didn't stop there, small children (underage) were also allowed to come and vote.

Poverty was seen as the crux of the problem; as one observer in Bauchi LGA in Bauchi put it, 'How could somebody with an empty stomach come for voting?' Even those in employment were suffering, 'some not having received their January salaries so they would readily jump at any offer of money for little favours even if it is unpatriotic. The Electoral Officers and security officials fall into this category of people' (this according to an observer in Jere LGA in Borno). But poverty itself had other ramifications, for instance the farmer in Misau LGA in Bauchi who told an observer that 'if he will participate in the election his family will starve for the day so he prefer [sic] meeting up with his family obligations rather than voting'. The women in Ihitte/Uboma LGA in Imo 'were hanging around the village square with their wares anxious to start trading'. Saturday was market day at Ganye LGA in Adamawa and 'everybody was very busy buying and selling at the market instead of going out to exercise their civil rights'. Conversely, youths in Yenagoa LGA in Bayelsa 'forcibly took away the ballot box and electoral materials, on the excuse that the politicians did not give them money'.

The police themselves were not left out of the bonanza; some of them were apparently satisfied with ₦100 to look the other way, although duplicity among thieves threatened to unravel at least one deal in a polling station in Nsukka LGA in Enugu:

Right there in my presence, they gave the policemen their own share of the money (N700) b/c they were seven in number. But, after, they discovered that the party agent brought N17,000 and the 'Honourable' has cheated them.

So they weren't where they were supposed to be but on their own looking for their share of the money.

In Igueben LGA in Edo: 'Police Comm. (rtd) threatened myself and my co-observer to play by the rules or we regret our visit to the polling station.' In Port Harcourt, capital of Rivers State, the observer 'overheard Inspector of Police Sir E K_ discussing openly with Mr. H_ . . . on how they (the police) put some ballot paper into the ballot boxes if he (Mr. H_K_B_) will go and bring the money'.

At one polling station in Biase LGA in Cross River, 'the Presiding Officer, the polling clerk and four other men did the thumb pr[i]nting'. In Udu LGA in Delta, 'the accreditation was done without voters present by the presiding officer and the PDP agents who now engaged themselves in massive thumb-printing which they now kept in the ballot box'. In Etsako West LGA in Edo, 'the PDP and presiding officer were putting the ballot paper in the ballot box'. In Èkìtì South West LGA in Èkìtì, 'those that were accredited were 10 in number but the presiding officer said it was 333'. In Nkanu East LGA in Enugu, 'the presiding officer gave the number of accredited voters as 23 but to my greatest surprise the election results were returned as follows: PDP 400, APP 20'. In Jema'a LGA in Kaduna, 'Seventy-four people were accredited and voted, but the presiding officer and his clerk sold three hundred and one (301) ballot papers to PDP.' In Matazu LGA in Katsina, 'The PDP officials, APP, security and the presiding officer colluded and rigged 508 ballot papers.' In Asari-Toru LGA in Rivers, 'The boxes were kept under benches and some used as seats while officials occasionally open and pour in as much ballot paper as they could thumb print and pour into the ballot boxes.'

At the most extreme, everybody simply retired to the chief's compound. In Brass LGA in Bayelsa, 'I waited until

5:30 p.m. and there was no sign of election, as everyone was going on with their normal businesses. We were later made to understand that all the material [was] taken to Chief Dura's house to INEC Yenagoa for submission.' In another polling station nearby, 'the materials were taken to an unknown place on the order of one Chief O. Abbey who influenced the officials with money'. There was a variation of the same in Gusau, capital of Zamfara, where the polling station was moved from its original site 'on the Main Road' to the front of a 'notorious political house headed by one rich politician in the person of I_ M_ in order to intimidate voters':

> By my critical observation [I] noticed and heard from voters the less privileged citizens in this station are fearful in one way or the other to vote the party of their own choice but a party favoured by the family. The situation is such that people are intimidated or harassed systematically without complaints from any member of INEC or security noticing or paying much attention. Members of the family do not form queue regularly and under aged female members of the family are allowed to vote without any questioning.

In all this chicanery, it was strange to come across state military administrators admonishing voters 'to conduct themselves with decorum', 'to follow the rules and regulations [given] to us', but two unrelated incidents exemplify the underlying hysteria in the country occasioned by the latest round of transition-without-end. The first involved an official of the state electricity company in Kaduna State who was 'seriously beaten by the crowds' before he was able to establish his credentials. They thought he was 'trying to derail the transition process'. The other involved 'a child [who went] missing' in Kaduna North LGA early in the morning on polling day. When news reached the polling station, voters became tense because they suspected 'that the child was missing for ritual purposes'. It happened to be on the eve of a 'certain traditional festival' in which fifty cows were to be slaughtered 'for sacrifices'.

Conversely, there were areas of calm amid the violence and insecurity, for instance the presiding officer in Kaduna North LGA in Kaduna who would not be corrupted:

> At around 11 am one female agent supervisor of the PDP approached the presiding officer for the release of 150 ballot papers which the presiding officer turn down her request and said to her: 'I will not release any ballot paper not even for 1 million naira will I do that.' The said agent supervisor tried her possible best to persuade the officer but to no avail, the presiding officer refused all her words and promises.

Or the INEC official in Mbaitoli LGA in Imo State who found himself out of pocket in order that he might fulfil his patriotic duty:

> When I arrived I saw that the people of the place was so rough on the INEC's officials as to providing tables and chairs.
>
> The presiding officer had to sweep the area by himself, even bring in tables and chairs. The first place he went the owner demanded for some money before she could release her table.

Ọbásanjọ́ duly won, a remarkably depressing feat given we should have forsworn the military in any guise, but that was nothing compared to what was to happen sixteen years later when, astonishingly, the Nigerian electorate did the same again and voted in Muhammadu Buhari, he of the retroactive decrees and imprisonment for writing the truth. Then again, you can hardly have bad leadership without bad followership even allowing for the fact that the returns for the 1999 elections were greatly influenced by 'stomach infrastructure' – that is, hunger – a term coined during the 2014 gubernatorial by-election in Èkìtì State, as we shall see in the next chapter.

4

The Dividends of Democracy; or, How Not to Move the Nation Forward

No, I am not interested in becoming the head of state again.
Besides, I am a retired professional soldier. Civilians should
elect the leaders they want to become their President.
                                        – General Olúṣẹ́gun Ọbásanjọ́

Age is telling on me. Working for six, seven hours a day is
no joke. I asked for it and I am not expecting any appreci-
ation from Nigerians. What I expect is for Nigerians to say,
'This man has done his best.'
                                        – General Muhammadu Buhari

The first to discover that the military had simply swapped khaki for agbádá were the people of Choba, a city half an hour's drive from Port Harcourt. The problem started when Wilbros, a Shell contracting company, declined to honour a memorandum of understanding with the community and instead made a deal with selected chiefs. As happened during a previous confrontation, the community staged a peaceful demonstration, this time by blocking the gates to the company and stopping all vehicular movement. Regular and mobile police were drafted in, to be followed, three days later, by soldiers. A national newspaper subsequently published four photographs of two women being flogged and raped. I have the images before me as I write. The first shows one of the women being beaten. The second shows that same woman being raped. The third shows the other woman being beaten. The fourth shows her also being raped. Both soldiers are in full battle dress, one in a floppy hat, the other with a bandanna around his head. One of the victims said that because she was raped in public, 'I cannot hide it anymore.'

Next in line was Odi in neighbouring Bayelsa State, home of the 1999 Kaiama Declaration which rejected 'the fraudulent contraption' called Nigeria. The problem started when a gang of youths abducted and murdered seven police officers. Five more were killed over the next few days. Ọbásanjọ́ wrote the governor, Chief Diepreye Alamieyeseigha (who was to later sneak out of the UK dressed as a woman, of which more presently), criticising him for failing to take action and threatening to declare a state of emergency if the killers were not apprehended. Four days before the deadline, a heavily armed column of about 2,000 troops advanced on the town and was ambushed by the gang. Enraged, the soldiers razed the town over the next fortnight, leaving just three buildings standing: a bank, a church and a health centre. Dozens of people were killed and over 15,000 rendered homeless. Ọbásanjọ́'s special assistant on media and publicity lambasted critics of what happened as 'either guilty of shameful ignorance or simply playing to the gallery', but the spokesperson for the Second Amphibious Brigade underlined the brutality of Operation Hakuri 11, as it was called: 'The intention was just a show of force, to let them know they cannot continue like that . . . No village will want to go through what that village went through. It has been taught a lesson.' As for Ọbásanjọ́:

I served in that part of the country during the Nigerian civil war. I am very familiar with the problems of the area.

I toured the Niger Delta extensively during my election-eering campaign and gave my word that the area deserves a properly articulated blueprint for its development.

It is because of my concern about the underdevelopment of the area that I visited the Niger Delta within the first two weeks after my inauguration as President. Soon after that, we presented a bill to the National Assembly on the Niger Delta. All these efforts were geared towards reassuring the people of the area that they occupy a very special place in the national scheme, and indeed in the development agenda of our administration.

People now behead their fellow kinsmen, laying ambush and murdering law enforcement agents. They resort to piracy, hijacking oil vessels on the high seas, they loot, they steal, they burn down houses and whole communities. This is sheer nothing but criminality.

I will not condone criminal acts. Anyone found to have run foul of the law by committing any of these atrocities will be apprehended and punished, irrespective of their status in society.

I have said it over and over again, and I will keep repeat-ing this warning, that our administration will not spare sacred cows. Anyone who has contributed in any way to the unrest in the Niger Delta will not go unpunished.[1]

As a 'Western' journalist noted at the time, 'The operation was so brutal that had an army leader, rather than the new civilian president, been responsible, it would have pro-voked worldwide outrage.'[2]

---

1 J. O. Obari, 'Federal government deploys troops in Bayelsa', *Guardian*, 27 November 1999.

2 Karl Meier, *This House Has Fallen: Nigeria in Crisis*, London: Allen Lane, 2000, 142.

Perhaps Ọbásanjọ́ was anxious to prove his credentials to his northern masters and perhaps they took note, but if so they further underlined his impotence by immediately adopting Sharia law across all the northern states, an issue that had never before been on anybody's agenda. Since the time of colonisation, Sharia law had been limited to civil matters only – marriage, divorce, succession – and only between parties who were themselves Muslims. Criminal matters were the preserve of the common law courts inherited from the British. Moreover, in acknowledgment of the country's diversity, Section 10 of the 1999 Constitution followed the previous ones in forbidding the adoption of any religion as a state religion, even as the Supreme Court has consistently refused to give a ruling on the matter. For his part, the then attorney general and minister of justice, Chief Bọ́lá Ìgè, also a Christian southerner, circulated a letter to the relevant governors declaring it illegal on the grounds that it infringed on the rights of Muslims themselves by subjecting them 'to a punishment more severe than would be imposed on other Nigerians for the same offence', but this was just so much English, as we say, and hardly the point. Ọbásanjọ́ himself lamely opined that the agitation for full Sharia law would soon 'fizzle out'.

By the end of 2001, twelve northern states – Bauchi, Borno, Gombe, Jigawa, Kaduna, Kano, Katsina, Kebbi, Niger, Sokoto, Yobe and Zamfara (along with some local government areas in other states) – had enacted a wide range of legislation aimed at particular 'social vices' and 'un-Islamic behaviour': drinking alcohol, gambling, prostitution and 'excessive' mixing of unrelated males and females. To date, only the poor have suffered the consequences, beginning with Safiya Husseini and Amina Lawal, two women who became pregnant in the absence of their estranged husbands and were sentenced to death by stoning. Both were ultimately acquitted on a technicality although the alleged father of Husseini's baby didn't have to do anything more than protest his innocence in the absence of four male witnesses who were otherwise required to have seen 'the penis inside the woman's vagina'; as the judge put it, 'a man is not a woman, whereby she will have a protruding stomach to show.' In Lawal's case, the local government worker everyone in the village knew to be sweet on her, and who insisted they had done nothing more than hold hands – 'Yes, I agree that she was my girl-friend but I never had any sexual intimacy with her' – even declared himself willing to cast the first stone: 'I cannot plead for her pardon because I will be going against the law of Allah ... Since she was found guilty and already a death sentence has been passed, it should be executed as directed.' He allowed that she was 'a nice woman' who was merely 'unfortunate' in having had this happen to her. This declaration infuriated her younger brother, as who should know: 'The man was declared innocent because he swore on the Holy Koran. There is no truth in it. Now there is a death sentence hanging on the neck of my sister, while the man who impregnated her has gone scot-free.'

According to a retired chief magistrate, the main problem with the area courts, which account for about 80 percent of all cases in the North, 'is ignorance of applicable laws and procedure', and this is so 'especially in criminal matters', along with 'interference by the Inspectorate Section of the High Court and poor conditions of service'.[3] This was glaringly apparent in one pathetic early case in which two lovers were sentenced to death by stoning after

---

3 Anselm Chidi Odinkalu, *Justice Denied: The Area Courts System in the Northern States of Nigeria*, Lagos: Civil Liberties Organisation, 1992, 8.

the father of the pregnant woman, angered by her boy-friend's refusal to do the decent thing, took the matter to the authorities. His daughter was now 'spoiled', and he was eager that the fellow pay the price. The police got their confession but then everything went horribly wrong when the judge, applying what he presumed to be the letter of the law, sentenced both parties to five years' imprisonment or a fine of ₦15,000 (£75), and then, a fortnight later, changed his mind and sentenced them both to death, apparently in line with the new Sharia law. The distraught father, who claimed to have bribed the judge, could only leave 'everything to God. They should release my daughter for me. I thought that the court was going to solve the problem ... but, instead, it has spoiled it.' The judge, who refuted the allegation of bribery, had little sympathy: 'I believe he knew what he was saying and the consequences. His head is correct. I asked the boy too whether his head was correct and he said yes. I also asked ... Fatima and she said her head was correct.' Besides, he pointed out, 'igno-rance of the law is no excuse,' yet his own familiarity with the law left much to be desired. In the first place, Section 388 of the Penal Code, which deals with extramarital sexual intercourse, stipulates 'imprisonment for a term which may extend to two years or a fine or both'. In the second place, it was illegal for the same judge to retry his own case in the absence of a judicial review.

To date, nobody has been stoned to death, but two con-victed thieves had their right hand amputated, one for stealing a cow, the other for stealing three bicycles. In the case of the first, a surgeon was specially flown in from Pakistan because, it seems, no Nigerian doctor was availa-ble. The operation was performed at the state house clinic in Gusau, the capital of Zamfara State, as an excited crowd waited outside, whereupon the amputee was led back to his impoverished village by state government officials in what was described as a festive atmosphere. However, the imposition of Sharia generated unrest in 'front-line' states, Kaduna in particular, which is more or less evenly divided between the religions. Riots erupted over the state's hosting of the 2002 Miss World competition, triggered by a newspaper article that suggested the Prophet himself would have approved the presence of the beauty queens and perhaps chosen a wife or two from among them, but that was just an excuse. A fatwa was issued against Isioma Daniel, a journalist, who was forced to flee the country. Over two hundred people died.

It happened that at the time I had the opportunity to travel across the nine core northern states and saw for myself the extent of Saudi influence. In Sokoto, seat of the Caliphate, the state government was given £2.6mn to build an Institute for Koran and General Studies, which was opened by the chief Imam of the Grand Mosque at Mecca, Sheikh Abdulrahman Al-Sudais, who confirmed that 'Saudi authority is behind the Institute and will do everything possible to upgrade its standard.'[4] It's possible the Saudis were also behind the colleges of Islamic Legal Studies in all the states I visited, yet few of the governors were ready to adhere to the Agenda for Action spearheaded by Atiku Abubakar, the then vice president, in allocating 26 percent of their budget to education, which is why the North currently has the highest number of out-of-school children in the world, roughly three-quarters of the 20 million nationwide, more even than India, second to Nigeria but with over six times our population. As I wrote at the time:

---

4 Adewale Maja-Pearce, 'Diary', *London Review of Books*, Vol. 24, No. 24, 12 December 2002.

The result can be seen in the motor parks of the state capitals, where the al-Majiris, teenage boys attached to Koranic teachers, go about begging for their daily bread. These boys, who are required to learn the Koran by rote in Arabic, a language that isn't spoken in Nigeria, usually hang around in groups of a dozen or so, barefoot and in rags, or trail behind a teenage female hawker in search of devout travellers anxious to fulfil the Islamic injunction on charity. The girls themselves, some as young as 12, with kohl-rimmed eyes and painted lips that flash gold whenever they smile, sell more than bean cakes, sugar cane and oranges. One of them, Bariya Ibrahim Magazu, was charged in Zamfara with engaging in premarital sex and bringing false accusations against three men she said had slept with her. She was found guilty and sentenced to 180 lashes. The punishment was administered before her appeal was heard, despite the lack of a 'protruding stomach to show' and in the absence of even one of the men she was supposed to have slept with.

One perverse feature of the Islamist obsession over who is having sex with whom and why, is the lack of concern about Aids, to say nothing of unwanted pregnancies, which are flourishing in Nigeria. It doesn't take long to notice the scarcity of billboards advertising condoms, while the publicly funded radio stations are apparently forbidden to inform their listeners about the advantages of safe sex. I was told this would only encourage men to patronise 'illegal' women, which was un-Islamic, like so much else.[5]

In contravention of the National Broadcasting Commission rules, daily readings from the Koran occupied well over 10 percent of airtime. Not every journalist liked what

---

5   Ibid.

was happening but they had little choice: there were no alternative radio stations and the few existing weekly newspapers – one each in Sokoto, Kebbi and Zamfara – were dedicated to the re-election of the state governor. In Gusau, capital of Zamfara, the first state to adopt Sharia under Governor Ahmad Sani Yerima (he with the predilection for little girls, as noted in the preface), the only multistorey building was the Ministry of Religious Affairs, a ministry tasked with ensuring strict adherence to the party line and complete with an Office of the Moon Sighting Committee which stirred up all the fuss about the Miss World competition, although the office was closed just then because we were still a fair way from the Ramadan that had coincided with the event. A bearded information officer in a flowing white robe told me he was on holiday from a university in Saudi Arabia before handing me a selection of pamphlets. One was by a former Christian from Canada, a fact that was loudly flagged. His topic was whether it was permissible for a woman to show her hands and face in public. Being Canadian, he came down firmly on the side of the liberals, although it would be interesting to have his take on the 2022 demonstrations in Iran following the death of a young woman for not wearing her headscarf just so.

Unfortunately for the governors (to say nothing of the country), the introduction of Sharia law had the unintended consequence of fuelling an Islamic insurgency now that the genie had been released. Most people first heard about Boko Haram when they kidnapped 276 girls from a boarding school in the town of Chibok in Borno State in the far North-east on the night of 14–15 April 2014, sparking the hashtag #BringBackOurGirls spearheaded by Oby Ezekwesili, a former education minister and World

Bank vice president for Africa, who organised a sit-in at a national park in Abuja. The cry was taken up by celebrities around the world, including Michelle Obama, the then US First Lady, who was photographed holding up a placard. As it turned out, it was only by chance that the girls were in the school that day; schools were out for the holidays, but these girls had returned to sit a physics exam. As it also turned out, the terrorists had only left their hideout in Sambisa Forest – a huge national park long since fallen into the usual neglect – in search of food and fuel. Meeting no resistance from the soldiers stationed nearby, they broke into the school and rounded up the girls when they had finished looting. A few of the captives managed to jump off the back of the trucks as they entered the forest and were taken in by small farming communities; the rest were distributed among the 'Soldiers of Allah' as 'wives'.

Boko Haram, which roughly translates as 'Western education is forbidden', was actually founded in 2002 by an obscure preacher by the name of Mohammed Yusuf, who called upon 'the Muslim community to correct its creed and its behaviours and its morals', 'to give children a correct Islamic education' and 'to undertake jihad in the name of Allah'. As the sect further explained in a 2009 pamphlet, secular education leads to 'Western Ways of Life', including 'the rights and privileges of women, the idea of homosexuality, lesbianism . . . rape of infants, multi-party democracy . . . drinking beer and alcohol and many other things that are opposed to Islamic civilisation'. This was obviously a challenge to the state governors who were agitating for full Sharia law for political reasons but who had no problem sending their children to elite schools abroad, along with the rest of the Hausa-Fulani aristocracy, including the Sultan of Sokoto, President Buhari and Mallam Adamu Adamu, all of whom were proudly photographed alongside their children on graduation day from one or another British university. As chance would have it, Adamu also happened to be minister for education at a time when federal universities were on a prolonged strike. When asked about his sojourn in the UK during a meeting with the National Association of Nigerian Students, his response was to storm out. At least one newspaper editorial called his behaviour 'unbecoming and immature'.[6] He later resigned, saying he had been a failure over his inability to fulfil a promise to reduce the number of out-of-school children by half before the end of his tenure, which he called 'a big mark of shame to him as a person and to the entire nation'.[7] He further claimed to have poured billions of naira into the sector but then a British education is not cheap.

Boko Haram's founder Yusuf was a university graduate himself – he had studied theology in Medina – but his calls for jihad were vague and adapted for the occasion; he is described as 'a dynamic, even chameleon-like preacher' who 'presented his ideas in different ways to different audiences'.[8] But he was evidently popular. One eyewitness recounted his triumphant return to Maiduguri following one of his brief detentions: 'People came all the way from Kaduna, Bauchi and Kano to welcome him. There was a long motorcade from the airport as thousands of his members trooped out to lead him to his house. He came back like a hero.'[9] Some among them were obviously

---

6 'Adamu's walk-out on protesting students', *Vanguard*, 4 March 2022.

7 Adamu Adamu, 'My successes, failure as Nigeria's education minister – Adamu', *Premium Times*, 22 May 2019.

8 Alexander Thurston, *Boko Haram: The History of an African Jihadist Movement*, Princeton: Princeton University Press, 2017, 83.

9 Ibid., 131.

well-heeled: whenever he preached in his large compound in Railway Quarters, 'the whole area would be lined with exotic cars as very powerful individuals came to see [him]. They went in cars with tinted glass.'[10] Among them was the then Borno State governor, Ali Modu Sheriff, widely rumoured to be the founder of Boko Haram (which he vehemently denies), who was obliged to woo Yusuf in his bid for the state governorship in 2003. Once in office, Sheriff appointed Yusuf to a committee selecting Muslims to take part in the annual Hajj to Saudi Arabia, but the arrangement didn't last long. By then Sheriff was preoccupied with party political issues playing out in Abuja, and Yusuf's extremism was becoming an embarrassment.

Indeed, Yusuf came to believe that Sheriff had turned against Boko Haram in the wake of his successful 2007 re-election bid. The following year, Sheriff unleashed Operation Flush, a military sweep whose official raison d'être was to curb banditry in the state's hinterlands. The next year, soldiers opened fire on a procession of unarmed Boko Haram members on their way to a funeral on motorbikes in a town outside Maiduguri. (According to the military, they weren't wearing helmets, as required by law.) In response Yusuf decided to launch his insurrection, declaring: 'We are ready to die together with our brothers.'[11]

The uprising was initially slated for August 2009 but two events brought it forward. On 23 July, the authorities discovered a 'training camp' in Biu in Borno State and arrested nine. The following day, Boko Haram members accidentally detonated a bomb in a safe house in Maiduguri. With their cover blown, Yusuf gave the go-ahead:

---

10 Ibid., 89.

11 Quoted in Virginia Comolli, *Boko Haram: Nigeria's Islamist Insurgency*, London: C. Hurst & Co., 2015, 54.

On 26 July, around seventy Boko Haram members 'armed with guns and hand grenades' attacked a police station in Bauchi. Police repulsed them, killing several dozen and arresting an estimated two hundred sect members; arrests went well beyond just the fighters and extended to the sect's wider membership in the city. In Potiskum, Yobe [State], a 'gun battle raged for hours' around a police station; police arrested twenty-three people. A small clash occurred between Boko Haram and police in Wudil, Kano State. On 27 July, severe battles paralysed Maiduguri. Boko Haram staged a 'co-ordinated late-night assault on the state's police headquarters, police training facilities, Maiduguri prison, and two other police stations'. Further battles happened in Gamboru-Ngala in Borno, near the border with Cameroon – a town that would become a flashpoint later. 'Heavily armed members of the sect stormed the town and went on the rampage, burning a police headquarters, a church and a customs post.'[12]

On 28 July the military shelled Yusuf's home at Railway Quarters, where some sect members had 'barricaded themselves in and around the house after heavy fighting'. Yusuf was found the next day, 'hiding in a goat pen at his parents-in-law's house'. He was interrogated by soldiers and then handed over to the police, who executed him in public – you can see it on YouTube – as an ecstatic crowd looked on. They later executed his father-in-law.

Yusuf's mantle now fell on one Abubakar Shekau. Like Yusuf, he belonged to an extremist Salafi sect, the Society for the Removal of Heretical Innovation and the Establishment of the Prophet's Model, which held that Muslims who strayed from the path were fair game, but he also

---

12   Thurston, *Boko Haram*, 136–7.

seemed to be unbalanced, at least in the more conventional sense. He once boasted on social media that he enjoyed 'killing anyone that God commands me to kill the way I enjoy killing chickens and rams'. According to at least one account, the death in childbirth of one of his wives 'triggered some existing but hitherto repressed psychiatric problem: he became so violent that it was necessary to put him in chains'. At the time of the Chibok kidnappings, he claimed that the girls were slaves and would be sold in the market because 'Islam permits slavery.'

Where Yusuf had limited the sect to bombing government property, Shekau turned his attention to churches, mosques, banks, markets and schools in what was described as 'total war' in north-eastern Nigeria, beginning with the suicide bombing of the Nigeria Police headquarters in Abuja in June 2011 (the first such attack in Nigerian history), followed, six months later, by the Christmas Day suicide bombings of three churches, one of them across the border in Niger. The insurgency peaked between 2009 and 2015, with the loss of some 20,000 civilian lives.[13] In 2014, it declared its 'capital' in Gwoza, Borno State (it lasted just seven months) and affiliated with IS, rebranding as 'Islamic State in West Africa' or 'Islamic State West Africa Province'. It expanded its use of suicide bombers, mostly young women and girls, including a ten-year-old.

Unwittingly or not, Boko Haram's ascendancy gave the fillip to Buhari's presidential ambitions in the 2015 elections, the very year that the National Intelligence Council, an American think tank, prematurely predicted the 'outright

---

13   The actual figure, according to the UN, 'is likely to be much higher'. 'Violations and abuses committed by Boko Haram and the impact on human rights in the countries affected', Report of the United Nations High Commissioner for Human Rights, 9 December 2015, 6.

collapse of Nigeria'. The incumbent, Goodluck Jonathan, a Christian southerner, was deemed to have failed woefully over the terrorism threat, especially after the kidnapping of the Chibok girls the previous year. Indeed, it took him more than two weeks to call a press conference, where he looked awkward in military fatigues and answered a reporter's question with, 'I don't know where they are . . . there is no confirmation of the location of the schoolgirls, you are a journalist, you know more than me.'

As the election drew near, he stirred into action, agreeing that Chad, Cameroon, Niger and Benin could deploy their own troops inside Nigeria as the insurgency began to spread beyond the country's borders. However, Idriss Déby, the president of Chad, complained, 'We've been on the terrain for two months, and we haven't seen a single Nigerian soldier. There is a definite deficit of co-ordination and a lack of common action.' Jonathan also engaged a firm of mercenaries run by a former South African Defence Force officer, Eeben Barlow, who was even blunter: 'Foreign armies . . . have spent considerable time in Nigeria where "window-dressing training" has been the order of the day. But look through the window and the room is empty.' A 'senior Western diplomat' (are there never any senior non-Western diplomats?) told the *New York Times* that the mercenaries were playing 'a major operational role' carrying out night attacks on Boko Haram and that 'the next morning the Nigerian army rolls in and claims success'.

To nobody's surprise, it later transpired that money intended for the military was being embezzled: Jonathan's chief security adviser, Sambo Dasuki, was accused of stealing US$2.1bn. (He must have stepped on a great many toes because he was to be detained by the Buhari administration for four years in contravention of Section 35 of the Constitution, which allows for only forty-eight hours.)

According to Transparency International, 'corrupt senior officers withheld ammunition and fuel from frontline soldiers, leaving them with no alternative other than to flee when attacked.' When the army did venture out, its reputation was further tarnished by its behaviour towards villagers in combined operations with the Civilian Joint Task Force (a dubious initiative started by local youths in 2013 to identify Boko Haram suspects and get them to 'confess'). A report by Amnesty International alleged there was 'compelling evidence of widespread and systematic violations of international humanitarian and human rights law by the military, leading to more than seven thousand mainly young Nigerian men and boys dying in military detention and more than 1200 people killed in extrajudicial executions'. According to the report, 'no one was brought to justice'.

Following his election victory, Buhari immediately moved the centre of operations north to Maiduguri and allocated more resources but the tide had already turned. He was not entirely wrong in declaring that Nigeria had 'technically won the war' against the sect in 2015, or in announcing its 'final crushing' one year later. Even so, it wasn't the whole truth. The military has confined its members to the countryside, mainly the inaccessible mountainous areas on the border with Cameroon, where they continue to rampage with diminishing results. As Jama'atu Nasril Islam, the umbrella body of Nigeria's Muslim community, has said, there is good reason to suspect that the security forces have been colluding with the remnants of the movement in order to keep counterinsurgency funds from Abuja flowing their way.

It happened that I travelled by road from Abuja to Maiduguri in late 2017, twelve hours in all, where I took the opportunity to visit Chibok; as I wrote at the time, it was 'a journey I wouldn't have contemplated just two years earlier' (or since, for reasons already alluded to):

> I couldn't get to Gwoza, Boko Haram's former capital – a five-hour drive south-east from Maiduguri: Boko Haram may have been in retreat, but there had been no 'final crushing' and the roads were still unsafe. I couldn't do the three-hour drive south to Chibok either: some lecturers from a local university had recently been abducted. But I did make a 14-hour roundabout journey to the town, with many military checkpoints along the way. It turned out that the story wasn't in Chibok any longer. But if I hadn't made the trip I might never have understood that the kidnapping of the schoolgirls in 2014 is now a slow-burn revenue source, not just for the military, but for numerous NGOs: this once insignificant town is full of white four-by-fours, driven by aid workers.[14]

But the greater threat to the stability of the country as a whole and not just the North is a group known as Fulani herdsmen, cattle-rearing descendants of Usman dan Fodio's 1804 jihad driven south by desertification following the ravages of climate change.[15] According to the Global Terrorism Index, in 2016 they 'undertook more attacks and

---

14   Adewale Maja-Pearce, 'Where to begin? After Boko Haram', *London Review of Books*, Vol. 40, No. 8, 26 April 2018.

15   According to a 2021 report from the World Economic Forum, climate change 'is already wreaking havoc across the region', with temperatures in the Sahelian strip 'rising 1.5 times faster than the global average' and 'worsening the region's existing issues of droughts, desertification and erosion'. As for Nigeria, the report estimates that as many as nine million citizens 'could be pushed to migrate in some of the country's most vulnerable regions unless early action is taken by the government'.

were responsible for more deaths than Boko Haram', hence everyone's wariness when we came across a group of them during my journey:

> We were held up for an hour while a party of Fulani crossed the road to a muddy watering hole, the men in wide-brimmed straw hats, loose trousers and plastic sandals, the women in bright dresses, with tightly braided hair and bangles on their arms, the boys and girls tall, dark and thin, driving their entire worldly wealth before them. My fellow passengers were uncharacteristically silent.[16]

This wasn't always so. From the mid-1990s until 2005, disputes involving Fulani pastoralists accounted for about 120 deaths in the North and Middle Belt but the group is now to be found in at least twenty-one of the thirty-six states, their bows and arrows replaced by AK-47s. According to the latest figures, between 2017 and May 2020 these herdsmen carried out 654 attacks in which 2,539 people were killed and 253 kidnapped. Here is a typical example from September 2022 at Logo LGA of Benue State:

> It is a sad day for us here in Logo; armed Fulani herdsmen attacked Mchia, a settlement along Abeda-Anyiin road, just three kilometres to Anyiin the Logo LGA headquarters at about 10pm.
>
> 'They killed 12 people there and shot so many that are at the hospital at the moment. One cannot tell of their condition because they were severely wounded.
>
> 'The attackers did not stop there, they went inside to Mou village where they shot so many people and killed two on the spot. Many are also missing and unaccounted for.

---

16 Ibid.

'These attacks were unprovoked. At Mchia village the people actually saw the Fulani herdsmen and heard them speaking their language.

'They came with sophisticated weapons from Arufu settlement in Wukari LGA of Taraba state which shares the same border with our communities.

'The attack was totally unprovoked there was no conflict between them and the attacked communities. They just want to chase us away from our ancestral homes and take over, so that they can have free access to graze on our farms.'[17]

To some, President Buhari's apparent unwillingness to curb their activities was proof that they were actually foot soldiers for achieving his deranged dream of turning the entire country into an Islamic state. 'I will continue to show openly and inside me the total commitment to the sharia movement that is sweeping all over Nigeria,' he said in 2001 as he called for 'the total implementation of the sharia in the country'. In a subsequent interview, he announced that he was willing to 'die for the cause of Islam'; in another, that 'we are more than the Christians if you add our Muslim brothers in the west.' He was referring to the 40-million-strong Yorùbá who are equally divided between Islam and Christianity (often within the same extended families) after much of its territory was conquered by the 1804 jihad on their mission to dip the Quran in the Atlantic. Almost uniquely, however, religious tolerance is a point of principle in Yorùbá culture, where extremism of any kind is frowned upon even as some of the desperate politicians among them unsuccessfully attempted to fan the ethnic flames in the aftermath of the 2023 elections, as we shall see in the concluding chapter.

---

17   *Vanguard*, 22 September 2022.

To make matters even worse, there has also been a steep rise in banditry, mostly in the North although the related phenomenon of kidnapping for ransom has become a nationwide problem, so much so that in the last three years it is simply no longer safe to travel anywhere by road, even as airfares have skyrocketed. As I write, there is on average one kidnapping a day on the previously safe Lagos-Ìbàdàn expressway, possibly the busiest highway on the continent and the gateway to the rest of the country. Even travel by train – on the few rail lines there are – is to be avoided. On 28 March 2022, hundreds of passengers on the newly inaugurated Abuja-Kaduna railway were kidnapped by 'marauding bandits' on motorbikes carrying firearms, the third and by far worst such incident in the short time it had been running. According to eyewitness accounts, the train was bombed twice before the bandits opened fire on the passengers, killing up to fourteen, including Chinelo Megafu, a newly qualified medical doctor who tweeted as she lay dying, 'I'm in the train, I have been shot. Please pray for me.' About fifty-eight of the surviving passengers were abducted and taken into the bush. Their families were each told to pay ₦100mn ransom and they were freed as their families did so: one on 6 April, eleven on 11 June, seven on 9 July, five on 2 August, seven on 10 August, four on 19 August and the remaining twenty-three on 6 September.[18] In all, the bandits netted ₦6bn.

Most of the bandits operate in the North-west, in contrast to Boko Haram, which operates mostly in the North-east. According to an American journalist and researcher who spent time with bandits in Zamfara State in 2021, where they are largely concentrated, they number up to 30,000

---

18 Tinúbú used the occasion to donate ₦50mn but it's not clear whether some of this went to pay ransoms.

and range in age from nine ('shouldering a rifle the size of his torso') to forty, and are 'spread across dozens of gangs ranging in size from 10 fighters to more than a thousand'. Typical of those he interviewed was a fellow called Buhari (no relation to President Buhari and not the interviewee's real name in any case):

> Now nearing 30, Buhari was in his early 20s when a gang of fellow Fulani rustled his family's herd. He could not turn to the police, he says, since they would extort any herder who approached them. Semi-itinerant, often illiterate, their wealth tied up in a difficult-to-trace commodity, herders like Buhari are easy prey for rapacious officials, of whom there is no shortage in Nigeria.
>
> So, Buhari joined the gang that stole his herd in order to retrieve it. Besides, the security forces and local Hausa vigilantes had long been profiling him. Given this treatment, and given that many of his friends were joining gangs, he suggests with a self-conscious shrug that 'there was no reason not to become a bandit.'[19]

Some of the bandits 'have purely extractive relationships with the local populace: Give the bandit money, cattle, wives or boys for his gang, and he won't torch your village.' In others, 'the protection racket is more proto-state, as the bandit assumes responsibility for security, arbitration and the means of production in his region'. One such bandit, Dogo Gide, 'regulates farming through neo-feudal sharecropping arrangements'. Another, Turji, 'builds mosques in local villages while dispensing harsh justice against petty criminals'. Yet another, Dankarami, 'holds

---

19   James Barnett, 'The Bandit Warlords of Nigeria', *New Lines Magazine*, 1 December 2021.

court with local politicians, hearing their petitions like a Saxon king'.[20]

To date, an estimated 12,000 to 19,000 people have been killed by the bandits, 'though the true number could be higher; in 2020, nearly 1,000 civilians were killed and just under 2,000 kidnapped in Kaduna alone, which is the only state to publish regular data on the conflict'. The number of displaced 'is also difficult to gauge owing to the significant NGO presence on the ground and state governments' tendency to downplay the humanitarian crisis', although 'a partial tally of northwestern and north-central states from mid-2021 brings the number of displaced due to banditry and farmer-herder clashes to just below 750,000'.[21]

In truth, there have been no dividends of democracy in the more than two decades since the military formally left. On the one hand, the population has almost doubled between then and now (119.3 million in 1999; 218.5 million in 2022); on the other, more people are poor, with an estimated 63 percent of all Nigerians currently living in extreme poverty. Between 2000 and 2021, the naira depreciated by an average of ₦473.53 per year, or 994.4 percent in twenty-one years.[22] More recently, the fall has become more precipitate; one economist calculated that ₦1mn in November 2021 was worth just ₦350k exactly one year later. Currently, the unemployment rate stands at 9.79 percent, but even those who are employed barely earn the laughable ₦30k minimum wage. Given, as we have seen, that almost half the population is under the age of twenty-one, the number of Nigerians entering the job market is set

---

20 Ibid.
21 Ibid.
22 WorldData.info.

to soar over the next decade. The simple – or complicated – fact is that no civilian administration has done anything to evade the calamity that is almost upon us.

Take Ọbásanjọ́'s two terms which ended in 2007 despite his attempt to change the constitution allowing him to run for a third. His big idea was to fix the protracted power problem. To put it into perspective, at the time we generated 4,000 megawatts to South Africa's 34,000 for a population one-third of ours (but admittedly South Africa is far more industrialised, which tells its own story, but never mind). Over the course of eight years, and amid much fanfare, he awarded contracts to the tune of US$16bn and even rebranded National Electric Power Authority (aka Never Expect Power Always) as Power Holding Company of Nigeria (aka Problem Has Changed Name), yet by the end of the exercise there was little or no difference.

And then it transpired, in the course of public hearings in the House of Representatives, that very little of the money actually reached the contractors. Worse yet, nothing happened because nothing was meant to happen; as we were told by Chief Tony Anenih, Ọbásanjọ́'s minister of works and housing, when asked to account for the over ₦300bn voted for his ministry between 1999 and 2003 to attend to the nation's deteriorating road network: 'At Okene . . . I stopped to buy fuel on my way from Abuja. I bought some newspapers. One of them amused me. The headline was "Anenih in soup". I was wondering which pot can be big enough to cook me before I can become soup. At least not in Nigeria.'[23] He knew what he was talking about. An investigation by the Senate produced a

23 'Targeting Chief Tony Anenih – "Mr. Fix It"', *Sahara Reporters*, 17 July 2007.

report which was subsequently shelved 'indefinitely' after the subject was relieved of his post but then immediately given charge of the ports, second only to oil for revenue generation. Coincidentally, his wife was named minister of women affairs, a hitherto unknown post.

The levels of graft, impunity and sheer depravity under our supposedly democratic dispensation are shocking and too numerous to detail but a few examples will suffice. Leading the way were the state governors, who carried on like mini-gods. One of the most notorious was Ikedi Ohakim, governor of Imo State in the South-east from 2007 to 2011, who ran the state 'like a family business' with his wife and junior brother: 'When it comes to contracts, Emma Ohakim will ask the commissioners to sign and they must sign, without even reading what they are signing or even getting a copy to keep.'[24] He also removed all local council chairpersons and replaced them with sole administrators in order to divert the monthly local government allocations. In the words of one 'source': 'The sole administrators are puppets and rubber stamps.'[25]

The governor was further accused of assaulting people within the precincts of government house. Three cases in particular made headlines. One concerned a Catholic priest, Rev. Fr. Eustace Okorie, whose car was accidentally held up in the governor's convoy in Owerri, the capital, whereupon the governor ordered his security aides to take him to government house, where he was stripped to his underwear, interrogated and detained for two days.

The other, far worse incident took place on 24 January 2010 and involved a journalist who was 'abducted' by

---

24 'Governor Ikedi Ohakim's Looting Spree Continues', *Sahara Reporters*, 26 July 2010.
25 Ibid.

armed men and taken to the governor's office, where he was ordered to strip:

> At that point I knew that I was in danger, so I played along. As I was removing my clothes, Ohakim stood up from the office chair and came to me and forcefully removed my clothes.
>
> Another young man of about 33yrs wearing an ash coloured suit came into the Governor's office to assist Ikedi Ohakim completely remove my clothes. I became completely naked before Ikedi Ohakim in the office of the Governor.

After hitting him a few times with his fists, the governor went over to his desk and brought out a horsewhip, which he proceeded to assault him with:

> 'Ikedi Ohakim flogged, flogged and flogged me ruthlessly, heartlessly and without mercy. He kicked me several times without mercy.
>
> 'The pain was much. I cried, cried and called on Almighty God to come to my rescue. I must have received well over 120 strokes of koboko.
>
> 'My blood completely stained the rug in the Governor's office. I was in pains. I saw hell with my two eyes.
>
> 'Ikedi Ohakim continued to flog me. His brother Emma Ohakim walked in and said "Chineke, His Excellency, His Excellency".
>
> 'Ikedi Ohakim said to his brother, "Emma, this is Ikenna Samuelson. I will kill him today". Emma simply left the office.'

He said when the pains became unbearable, he grabbed Ikedi Ohakim's legs and pleaded with him reminding the governor that they were in-laws.

'He then shifted a chair and sat down with the koboko still in his hands,' he said, adding that the governor started to shout, "Samuelson you have disgraced me in this country. You have finished me. I will kill you and nothing would happen".[26]'

Samuelson was then handed over to the commissioner of police and locked in a cell. The following day, still in his blood-stained clothes, he was taken to court to answer charges of 'defamation' of character before a magistrate who had already been compromised by Ohakim with an offer to become a substantive judge:

> My lawyer Barrister L. M. Alozie requested that I pulled off my clothes for the court to see the wounds Ikedi Ohakim inflicted on me. Mrs. Victoria Isiguzo refused. My lawyer requested that I tell the court my ordeal in the hands of Ikedi Ohakim. Mrs. Victoria Isiguzo refused. My lawyer requested that I be taken to hospital for treatment for my wounds. Mrs. Victoria Isiguzo refused. Rather Mrs. Isiguzo remanded me in Owerri Prisons custody for 8 days obviously to allow my wounds to heal and deny the general public to see my fresh wounds.

He was finally granted bail on 2 February 2010 and pursued the matter on his own behalf but only ended up back in prison for most of July for 'contempt' before agreeing to back down. His final recourse was to the 'court of public opinion'.

Then there was the case of a businessman, Sir Jude Uche Nkpado, who had answered the call to return home from the United States to contribute his quota to moving the nation forward. He claimed that on 1 April 2010, over

---

26 'Governor of Imo State, Ikedi Ohakim, flogged me – Samuelson', *Elombah.com*, 19 February 2010.

fifty armed men and about one hundred vigilantes stormed his printing plant, Excelsior Press Ltd. in Owerri, stole ₦3.7mn meant for salaries and destroyed equipment worth US$2mn. Seven members of staff were 'abducted' by the police. The plant itself was subsequently sealed up. The problem appeared to have been a book, *The Guarantee for Good Governance: Ohakim Must Go*, which the firm printed – perhaps unwisely – solely as a commercial venture.[27]

So why did the good people of Imo State put up with it? The answer was provided by Ayọ̀ 'stomach infrastructure' Fáyóṣé's victory in the 2014 gubernatorial by-election in Èkìtì State for a second term, after he had been impeached by the State House of Assembly for embezzling funds meant for a poultry project and forced to flee the country one year before the end of his first term (a feat indeed, of which more presently). He was also thought to have ordered the assassinations of some prominent political opponents in the state. Now he was back to challenge the incumbent, Káyọ̀dé Fáyẹmí, the London University PhD with solid credentials as a pro-democracy activist during the long, dark years of military rule, an official who had by now proved himself an able administrator: he built roads, ensured that pensioners received their due, and cleaned up corruption and incompetence in the public school system.

That Fáyóṣó was picked to contest a second time by the People's Democratic Party might appear as surprising as the fact that Fáyẹmí might lose, but Fáyóṣé won and by a wide margin – 200,000 to 120,000 – in a high turnout estimated at 71 percent of eligible voters. The first problem was Fáyẹmí himself. Put simply, he didn't carry the people

27 'Governor Ikedi Ohakim strikes again', *Nigerian Village Square*, 6 April 2010.

along. Like all the states in Nigeria bar Lagos, Èkìtì is predominantly rural and its people are far removed from the high-flown rhetoric at government house in the state capital. As one commentator put it, 'I cannot remember any newspaper that did not carry a long interview on his performance in government. His Twitter handle had a massive following and he was liked on Facebook.' Unfortunately, 'most of the farmers and teachers in Èkìtì State are not on Twitter or Facebook and do not read newspapers'. In short, 'the people in the grass-roots did not hear his message'.[28] Fáyóṣé, by contrast, was a man of the people. Again and again, those who voted for him talked about his common touch when he was governor the first time around, how he would stop his convoy to drink with the locals at a roadside bar, how he would escort the elderly into banks to help them open an account. As one jubilant voter put it, 'Fayose ate and drank with us, we love his simplicity, we love his style, he dined with us, we saw him on our streets in his shirts and shorts and could ask him for a handshake which he gladly obliged.'[29]

There was also the 'politics of the belly' as opposed to the 'politics of infrastructure', which was why Fáyóṣé himself coined the term 'stomach infrastructure'. It is difficult if not impossible to convince a hungry person that constructing roads and signing the Freedom of Information Act will benefit them in the long term. They want to eat, which was why Fáyóṣé campaigned with bags of rice purchased from Thailand, but, being Fáyóṣé, the rice had expired eight years earlier according to the Thailand Agency for Food Quality and Control. That Fáyóṣé was just then facing

28 Adewale Maja-Pearce, 'Thai Rice and Nigerian Politics', *New York Times*, 7 July 2014.

29 Ibid.

corruption charges, that is, charges for stealing their own money, didn't matter a jot, especially as everybody knew that his earlier impeachment was engineered by President Ọbásanjọ́ for personal reasons, and who was Ọbásanjọ́ – now out of power, hence Fáyọ́ṣẹ́'s return – to accuse anybody of corruption following his failed attempt to light up the country?

It stands to reason that not all governors were as bad. Even as Ohakim was flogging journalists and Fáyọ́ṣẹ́ was distributing expired rice, their counterpart in Jigawa State in the North-east, Sule Lamido, was widely praised for his stewardship, although it wouldn't have been difficult to outshine his predecessor, who apparently conducted government business from Hong Kong via telephone. Lamido, a disciple of the late Aminu Kano and his philosophy of service to the downtrodden, instituted the first social security bill in the country, under which every physically challenged person in the state – there were about 4,000 at the time – was paid ₦7,000 monthly. 'We, therefore, feel fulfilled that since June, the most deprived layer of the poor in this state no longer go to bed hungry on account of lack of money for the most basic requirement in this regard,' as he put it at the launching ceremony.[30] He also spoke out repeatedly against the culture of impunity which allows grand larceny to walk unchecked while oppressing the commoner:

> It is here in Nigeria that a corrupt office holder was arraigned before a court of law for corrupt practices and even pleaded guilty, but the person was set free and even elected a lawmaker to be promulgating laws to punish an

---

30 'The Game Changer and His Troubles', *TheNEWS Magazine* 17 January 2011.

ordinary thief of a goat or a pick-pocket. It is a shame and disgrace.[31]

For this reason, he advocated scrapping the immunity law from the constitution on the grounds that those who drafted it could not have imagined the thieves who would become governors. It is also on record that he was briefly detained under General Abacha for opposing the late dictator's self-succession plan, and although a loyal supporter of Ọbásanjọ́, who made him Minister of External Affairs in his first term, he categorically opposed his third-term bid.

But Lamido was the exception. More typical was Rivers State in the Niger Delta under Dr Peter Odili, which led to a damning report by Human Rights Watch, to wit:

> Rivers had a budget of $1.3 billion in 2006, larger than those of many West African countries, with a smaller population. But the state government has done little to alleviate poverty or improve the delivery of basic services ... At the same time, the governor of Rivers State budgeted tens of millions of dollars that year alone on questionable priorities like foreign travel, 'gifts,' and 'souvenirs' to unspecified recipients, and the purchase of jet aircraft and fleets of new cars for his office.

Pointing out that 'since the military left in 1999, democracy in Nigeria has been illusory, with elections stolen openly and voters systematically intimidated into acquiescence,' politicians in Rivers State have 'sunk even lower than these dismal norms', resulting in 'some of the worst socioeconomic indicators in the world – its people lack access to employment, education, health care, and other basic needs'.

---

31 'Freedom for Corrupt Public Officials Will Derail Growth – Sule Lamido', *Will*, 5 September 2010.

Worse yet, not only has the wealth been squandered; 'it has also been put to work sponsoring violence and insecurity on behalf of ruling party politicians':

> Prior to the 2003 elections, then-Governor Peter Odili and his political associates lavishly funded criminal gangs that helped rig the election into a landslide victory for the ruling [party]. Those gangs used the money at their disposal to procure sophisticated weapons; some of them are now better armed than the police.
>
> Over the years, gangs initially sponsored by Rivers politicians have become involved in other forms of lucrative criminal activity, including the theft of crude oil, bank robbery, kidnappings for ransom, and other violent crimes. In large part due to their political connections, these gangs have committed crimes with near-total impunity. The police have made no serious effort to press criminal charges against or apprehend any significant gang leader, even though several of them have lived openly in urban areas where their violent crimes resulted in murder and injury to ordinary Nigerians.[32]

One of the most powerful gangsters was Soboma George, who 'escaped from jail while awaiting trial for murder in 2005 but the police made no effort to re-arrest him'. Two years later, he was picked up on a traffic violation but 'armed men broke him out of a police station and he was again left untouched by police and law alike'.[33]

---

32 'Chop Fine: The Human Rights Impact of Local Government Corruption and Mismanagement in Rivers State, Nigeria', Human Rights Watch, 31 January 2007.

33 'Politics as War: The Human Rights Impact and Causes of Post-Election Violence in Rivers State, Nigeria', Human Rights Watch, 27 March 2008.

Matters weren't helped when the Supreme Court ruled in 2002 that it was unconstitutional and illegal to refuse to register only parties with national spread. By the time of the 2003 elections, thirty parties were registered, which proved a challenge to the electoral commission: 'It was a lot of system load for us. The ballot paper was about a metre long; it was certainly confusion for a lot of voters.'[34] By 2011, that number had risen to sixty-three; as another official from the commission put it, 'Is it not funny to you and laughable that 80 percent of the registered political parties are operating from hotel rooms, business centres and right inside the bedroom of their promoters as against the laid down rules.' In theory, opening up the political space was good if used to open up the democratic space. However, all it led to was confusion but with the two dominant parties still calling the shots even as they played musical chairs between them.[35]

An interesting point raised by the proliferation of parties was the tendency of the so-called radicals or progressives to form their own individual parties instead of coming together as a common front. One seasoned commentator put it this way while reflecting on Wọlé Ṣóyínká's emergence in 2011 as national chair of what the author himself doubted could even be called a political party, properly speaking:

The recent news that Wole Soyinka has decided to join partisan politics made headlines. The Nobel laureate, who was elected unopposed as chairman of the Democratic

34 'Guobadia to Jega: Take charge', *Guardian*, 18 October 2010.

35 Dare Adekanmbi, '2011: Hard times for political parties as INEC stops grants to them, halts registration of new parties', *Guardian*, 30 August 2010.

Front for a Peoples Federation (DFPF), also disclosed that the aim of the new party, which was initially denied registration in 2002, was to 'sanitize and transform Nigeria's nationhood into a democratic sanctuary for all her citizens'.

Soyinka's decision to embrace partisan politics raises a number of pertinent issues:

One, the new party raises a vital question of unity among the 'progressives', as it will now seem that virtually everyone of those often labelled by the press as 'progressive' – the late Gani Fawehinmi, Femi Falana, Pat Utomi, Balarabe Musa, Arthur Nwankwo and so on – is now the chairman (or is it the owner?) of a political party. This trend must be dispiriting for those hoping that the ascendancy of the 'progressives' in Nigerian politics will provide a genuine alternative to the current form of politics, which is often characterised by acrimony and disunity among the contending elites in their quest for power and lucre. If every 'progressive' must 'own' a political party – none of the founding chairman of these parties has ever stepped down or been voted out of office – it raises legitimate questions about the democratic credentials of the leaders of the 'progressive' camp.

While it is legitimate to criticise our traditional politicians who too often bombard the public space with the fallouts of their acrimonious intra-elite feuds for power and money, it is equally imperative that those who position themselves, or are seen as the alternatives to the traditional politicians, are very sensitive to the implications of their political conduct. For instance as the clamour for an alternative to the existing political order continues to get louder, with some even calling for a revolution, it could be legitimate to interrogate the implications of the tendency for each 'progressive' with a name recognition to carve out his own political fiefdom rather than work in concert with

others for democracy and national unity – should they
come to power.[36]

Regarding the parties themselves, there are regular complaints by aspirants that they lack internal democracy.
Candidates are imposed from above, even among so-called
progressive parties (relatively speaking, that is). A case in
point was the Action Congress of Nigeria, which was
regarded as the natural successor to Awólọ́wọ̀'s Action
Group and, later, Unity Party of Nigeria, which succes-
sively dominated the politics of the South-west. Cheated in
the 2007 gubernatorial election on its own turf by widespread rigging, it successfully challenged the results in the
courts. Following complaints of lack of internal democracy
within the party, its chair, Bisi Àkàndé, was unapologetic:

> If election within our party is what you are trying to
> describe as internal democracy, then we reject such idea.
> Can we impose when we are contesting against PDP? But
> we can do something within our party if the leadership of
> the party feels that that is the best thing. This is because it
> is the leadership of the party that understands the manifes-
> toes of the party *and knows what the people really want.*
>
> This is not a matter of an individual but the party. Nobody
> should accuse ACN of imposition because that is our style.
> Anyone that is not comfortable with that should go and
> contest in another political party. So if you see anyone carry-
> ing placard around, he is wasting his time. We know the
> efforts we made before the party became what it is today
> and where are they when we were making the efforts.[37]

36 Jideofor Adibe, email message to author, 29 September 2010.
37 Gbenga Olarinoye, 'Imposition of candidates is our style in ACN',
Vanguard, 20 January 2011. My emphasis.

Ironically, the second-largest party at the time, the All Nigerian People's Party, which grew out of the All People's Party whose national chairperson had told his people to rig the 1999 elections, was now the one observing the fundamental tenets of democracy, to wit:

> On the peaceful conduct of the primary election, Mallam Shekarau stated, 'I am truly proud to be associated with the ANPP, a party that has proved to Nigerians that there is still to be found in this country a party that is transparent, a party that is truly democratic, a party that respects every contestant, and a party that gives party members an equal chance to vote and to verify that one's vote counted. Our great party the ANPP has today showed that, in this country, there is still a party that does not employ intimidation or blackmail to get its way. Our great party the ANPP has today given every compatriot hope, that there is still hope for our country, a chance to turn things around; that there is still a chance to come together and move this country forward. Thank you ANPP for making us all proud, and for giving us satisfaction.'[38]

In fact, there is little to choose from between the parties, which is why those seeking office move freely between them. Take former president Buhari. He fought and lost both the 2003 and 2007 elections under the banner of ANPP, the second time vowing that if the results were not overturned within one month he would make the country ungovernable (they weren't and he didn't). He then left to form his own party, Congress for Progressive Change, to fight the 2011 elections, where he called on his followers in

---

38 Abdulaziz Abdulaziz, 'Now that Shekarau is ANPP Flagbearer', *Leadership*, 25 January 2011.

the North to police polling centres and 'lynch anybody that tries to tinker with the votes', an agitation that resulted in at least 170 Christians killed, many more injured and thousands displaced.[39] In 2015, he merged with the All Progressives Congress, an offshoot of the same Action Congress of Nigeria which didn't believe in 'internal democracy', and swore that 'by the grace of God, the dog and the baboon would all [sic] be soaked in blood' should he lose once more, so overweening was his sense of entitlement following his ouster a quarter-century before.[40] Fortunately for the animals at least, he finally won, in part helped by the support of public intellectuals, for instance Ṣóyínká, who had earlier compared him to a slave-driver but was now convinced that he was a genuine 'born-again democrat', although Buhari's wife, Aisha, suggested he was actually suffering from PTSD: 'You can imagine me at 19 years, handling somebody that went to war, suffered a coup d'état, then lost several elections . . . Also, for a woman to tell them that this is wrong or right in Nigeria and Africa is a problem.' She said that the experience caused her to become a physiotherapist. He, in turn, told her that her place was 'in ze kitchen and ze ozzer room'.[41]

However, lest anyone feel too sorry for her, she recently sprained her ankle while helping police from the Department of State Services flog a university student inside the Presidential Villa. It seems he had posted a comment on 'before' and 'after' photos showing her weight gain since becoming first lady, following which he was charged to court:

---

39   *Vanguard*, 16 June 2021.

40   *Vanguard*, 15 May 2012.

41   Sola Ogundipe & Chioma Obinna, 'Post Traumatic Stress Disorder: What experts said after Aisha Buhari's revelation', *Vanguard*, 15 October 2022.

That you Aminu Adamu, male of Anguwar Sarakuna, Bauchi, Bauchi state sometime between May – June 2022 within the jurisdiction of this Honorable court did intentionally open a Twitter Handle with the name @aminullahie Catalyst and screenshot the image of Her Excellency Hajia Aisha Buhari and wrote on it in Hausa language 'Su mama anchi kudi talakawa ankoshi' roughly translated to the English language to mean 'mama has embezzled monies meant for the poor to satisfaction' and posted same on your above Twitter handle for the members of the public to read, knowing same to be false and capable of affecting her reputation. You thereby committed an offence punishable under Section 391 of the penal code.[42]

He was initially remanded in custody for what was, in any case, a civil offense but then quickly released following a public outcry.

Buhari won again in 2019, this time against Atiku Abubakar, Ọbásanjọ's vice president from 1999 to 2007 and one of the three leading contenders come 2023. In theory, Atiku ought to have stood for the presidency back in the day, but he fell out with his boss when he refused to back his unsuccessful third-term bid and was replaced on the ticket by Musa Yar'Adua, nephew of Major General Yar'Adua, Ọbásanjọ's deputy as military ruler in the 1970s who was later killed by General Abacha. Musa Yar'Adua, who was sickly even as he entered office, died before he finished his first term, whereupon Goodluck Jonathan, his vice president, took over, as provided for by the constitution.

Jonathan then stood on his own account in 2011 and duly won before losing to Buhari in 2015. As I remarked

---

42 Sharon Osaji and Esther Blankson, 'JUST IN: Student sent to prison over Aisha Buhari tweet', *Punch*, 30 November 2022.

earlier, he lived up to his name. A zoology professor in a provincial university in his native Niger Delta, he had never dabbled in politics until he was drafted as deputy to Governor Diepreye Alamieyiseigha of oil-producing Bayelsa State in 2003. Two years later, he suddenly found himself governor when 'Alams' was impeached for money laundering to the tune of £12mn – £2mn in cash and accounts, £10mn in property – after being charged to court in the UK, whence he escaped dressed as a woman (in the process imitating Major Emmanuel Ifeajuna, one of the leaders of the 1966 coup who fled in the opposite direction but to Ghana similarly dressed). Jonathan was plucked from there to become Yar'Adua's running mate in 2007 on the grounds that he was a pliable fellow who would do as he was told (he pardoned his former boss as soon as he entered office), and thereafter assumed the presidency in 2010 following Yar'Adua's death.

Jonathan showed himself to be his own person when he refused to bow to the so-called zoning formula inserted into his party's constitution, whereby the North would serve out the second of its two four-year terms. Soon thereafter, four prominent northerners – including, incredibly, Ibrahim Babangida, the general who had *annulled* an election in order that his fellow coup plotter could judicially murder Ken Saro-Wiwa – also announced their intention to vie for the top slot at the party primaries. Eventually, Atiku (as he is commonly referred to, there being too many Abubakars) was selected and the others put their respective campaign machineries at his disposal, but at the party primaries Jonathan emerged the decisive victor, even defeating Atiku in his home state of Adamawa. According to reports, all the delegates were bribed by both campaign organisations; in the words of one:

On arriving Abuja, we got a call to meet with one of the presidential aspirants Atiku Abubakar in Minna. We went there and after some discussions we were given $2000 each. Back in Abuja, we were asked to go to our Governor's lodge. There we got another $7000. The money we were told was courtesy of Goodluck/Sambo campaign organization.

We learnt later that the money voted for the delegates by the two major contenders was more than what we got. We couldn't establish that but sources said the go-between or brokers, helped themselves with some part. The PDP governors backing the aspiration of the president were said to have contributed about ₦500 million. It is from this sum that they took care of the delegates from their respective states and the money was shared at the governor's lodges in Abuja.

I voted for Atiku at the convention to satisfy my conscience even though what I got from him was not as high as what I got from his opponent.

We got to know later that what the Atiku camp voted for the delegates was about $3000 each and what Jonathan camp voted was about $10,000, but something happened somewhere along the line. But what the delegates got each was less than this amount. Apparently, the middlemen had edited the sums.[43]

It seems that Jonathan's money came from Nigerian National Petroleum Corporation. The day after the primaries, Reuters reported that traders in the forex market said that transactions were short by about US$182mn due to a large cash withdrawal by NNPC, estimated at between ₦85bn and ₦90bn.

---

43 'Inside Nigeria's expensive presidential primary election', *Sunday Trust*, 23 January 2011.

Atiku took his defeat badly: 'As you all know, the convention fell short of our expectations,' he told members of his campaign organisation. 'You should not despair and on my own part, I want to assure you that I am not a quitter. If you think that I am quitting and giving up, you are making a mistake.'[44] True to his word, he was back again in 2019 and spent even more money under the banner of the People's Democratic Party that he had left following his fight with Ọbásanjọ́ over the self-succession plan but had now rejoined, and under whose banner he contested in 2023.

Atiku's personal fortune, which is reckoned at US$1.4bn (small beer compared to Tinúbú's), is the subject of much speculation, although he himself puts it down to luck and wise investments. What is certain is that he began acquiring it when he worked as a customs officer between 1969 and 1989, eventually rising to the rank of deputy director of the Nigeria Customs Service. During his eight-year stint as Ọbásanjọ́'s vice president, he was put in charge of the administration's IMF-inspired privatisation programme which was supposed to help deliver the 'dividends of democracy'. According to a US Senate report, between 2000 and 2008 Atiku and his fourth wife, who holds US citizenship, 'used a network of accounts at US financial institutions to bring over US$40mn in suspect funds into the United States, through multiple wire transfers supplied by offshore corporations located in Germany, Nigeria, Panama, the British Virgin Islands and Switzerland'. Some of that money came from his share of the US$12.7mn bribe paid by Siemens in exchange for telecommunications projects between 2001 and 2002. The sheer size of his war

---

44 'Presidential primaries: What is left for losers?', *Nigerian Tribune*, 27 January 2011.

chest was revealed at the PDP primaries ahead of the 2019 elections, where he outspent the other eleven hopefuls to the tune of ₦42bn (£8mn), but he was helpless against the incumbent, who had the resources of the state at his disposal. According to Governor Nyesom Wike of Rivers State, where Atiku was expected to do well, 'It was during the collation that operatives of the Nigerian army interfered. They will invade a collation centre, arrest the electoral officer, returning officer and mercilessly beat up the PDP agents.' Rótìmí Amaechi, the former governor and now a minister in the Buhari administration, was seen 'storming' an electoral commission office with one hundred soldiers in order to snatch ballot boxes. The point of the mayhem was to deter voters from leaving their homes. On election day, less than a fifth of the state's three million registered voters exercised their democratic right. A PDP agent lamented that his party 'could have captured more than a million votes' in the state. The pattern was repeated in the handful of northern states that favoured Atiku, for instance Zamfara in the North-west, where, according to the PDP, the military and mobile police overpowered party agents and altered the results in connivance with electoral commission officials to ensure a vote for the ruling All Progressives Congress (APC), under whose banner Asiwaju Bọ́lá Ahmed Tinúbú, the second of the three main contenders, fought in 2023.

The facts of Tinúbú's life are murky, beginning with his name. As I noted in the preface, his own purported family itself has denied him. Then there is his age. He claims that he was born in 1952, but that would mean he was just seven when he fathered his first child, Fọlásadé, who celebrated her sixtieth birthday in 2021 with all the fanfare of a self-respecting Yorùbá chief. (She now claims to be forty-six, having altered her Wikipedia page at least three times since then.) His education is also a matter of controversy. Nobody has been able to unearth which secondary school he attended. He once claimed to have graduated from the University of Chicago (which everybody had heard of) until the 'error' was discovered and it turned out he had meant Chicago State University (which nobody had heard of).[45]

What we do know is that he has a lot of money: US$32.7bn according to *Forbes*, much of it dating from his time as Lagos State governor. His fortune includes a fabulous property portfolio – he might just be the biggest landlord in the country apart from the federal government itself – but also a 10 percent cut of all Lagos tax revenue through his company, Alpha Beta Consulting, which he registered when he assumed office in 1999. Although he left in 2007 after his mandatory two terms, the company earned him US$176mn in 2021 alone. That he continues to enjoy a monopoly testifies to his stranglehold over state affairs, hence his nickname, 'the godfather', as he proved during the 2019 presidential election in Lagos State, where he unleashed violence spearheaded by his personal agbèrò, Musiliu Akínsànyà, aka MC Oluomo (among many other aliases). Until recently, Akínsànyà was also an executive of the National Union of Road Transport Workers, which collects 'fees' from drivers and traders at motor parks in all thirty-six states and constitutes a ready army of 'touts' at his disposal. He has never hidden his loyalty to his godfather: 'Anywhere his interest belong I, Musiliu Ayinde Akinsanya, MC Oloumo, belong.'

---

45   It is widely believed that his real name is Yekini Amoda Ogunlere, the name of someone who was apparently in a group photo in his primary school in 1947 in Iragbaji, in current Osun State, when he was nine years old. It is true that nobody has come out to confirm or deny his presence but it is likely that not many of his fellow students are still alive and those who are could have been easily 'settled' by someone who was to settle many Big Men in the 2023 elections.

A lengthy complaint by PDP agents from several polling stations described how 'hoodlums and miscreants led by Musiliu Akinsanya . . . took over the conduct of the election at the polling units . . . with arms and ammunition.' They carried other 'dangerous weapons such as machetes, charms and amulets', but the police made no attempt to arrest them. Independent observers backed up this statement, as does YouTube, where you can see said hoodlums and miscreants casually trashing ballot boxes while voters flee. As a result, Lagos reported the lowest turnout of any state at just 17 percent of almost seven million registered voters. As was to happen again in 2023, almost all this violence occurred in areas with a large Igbo population from the South-east who, as in Rivers State in the Niger Delta, would have voted for Atiku. Voting was otherwise largely peaceful in other areas, as I wrote at the time:

> In my own polling unit in a residential, solidly middle-class Yoruba-speaking area of Surulere in Lagos, a single unarmed policeman had very little to do while fifty or so citizens waited patiently under a canopy to cast their votes, without an agbero in sight. The polling officer and his assistant were both young. At the end of the exercise, which took longer than it should have because there was only one inkpad, the polling officer held up each ballot paper in turn for all to see as he tallied the votes. There was a small fracas over the number of voided votes, which necessitated a recount. People were understandably suspicious.[46]

Tinúbú is far from alone in his venality but doesn't feel compelled to hide it, perhaps because of his earlier

---

46 Adewale Maja-Pearce, 'Make Nigeria Great Again', *London Review of Books*, Vol. 41, No. 9, 9 May 2019.

straitened circumstances that he is so anxious to down-play. In the run-up to the 2019 presidential election, two bullion vans were seen entering the refurbished mansion he was gifted as part of his pension from a grateful Lagos State. When asked about the vans, he said that it was nobody's business but that, in any case, he needed to draw on his vast resources to ensure Buhari's victory since even the president 'doesn't have the type of money needed for Lagos votes'. This was the very same Tinúbú who once called Buhari 'an agent of destabilization, ethnic bigot and religious fanatic who, if given a chance would ensure the disintegration of the country', all of which are true (or about to be) but this is politics. At any rate, Buhari won his second term, earning Tinúbú the title of 'kingmaker' to add to that of godfather.

And now the kingmaker himself would be king even as he petulantly insists that it is his 'turn':

> If not for me that led the war front, Buhari won't have emerged. He contested first, second and third times, but lost. He even said on television that he won't contest again.
>
> But I went to his home in Katsina, I told him you would contest and win, but you won't joke with the matters of the Yorubas.
>
> Since he has emerged I have not been appointed Minister. I didn't get nor request a contract. This time, it's Yoruba turn and in Yorubaland, it's my tenure . . .
>
> '. . . It is my time, I'm educated, I'm experienced. I have been serving people for a long time, bring me the presidency, it is my turn.[47]

---

47   Eniola Daniel, 'Tinúbú says he went to "war" for Buhari to be president', *Guardian*, 2 June 2022.

However, by identifying so closely with Buhari during his re-election bid, Tinúbú alienated many of his own people, especially given that the incumbent's reign proved more disastrous than even his detractors feared. Nigeria is not working, hence the much-circulated photo of Buhari reclining in an easy chair, a contented look on his face as he picks his teeth, his shoeless feet crossed at the ankles. As the Africa editor for the *Financial Times* put it:

> The presidential election of February 2023 will draw the curtain on eight years of the administration of Muhammadu Buhari on whose somnolent watch Nigeria has sleepwalked closer to disaster.
>
> Buhari has overseen two terms of economic slump and a calamitous increase in kidnapping and banditry – the one thing you might have thought a former general could control.[48]

Now all the talk is of restructuring, of which Tinúbú was formerly an outspoken supporter – 'Our system remains too centralized, with too much power and money remaining within the federal might' – although he has since walked back on it. Now he merely says that the country is at a 'critical junction', that 'much work needs to be done', that we 'need to continue to transform and improve', which is why he is out of step with much of his own Yorùbá ethnic group. As we saw in the first chapter, he also alienated the young, the largest demographic by far, following the so-called Lekki Toll Gate massacre in October 2020, when soldiers opened fire on the peaceful #EndSARS protestors, killing twelve because they threatened his daily take-home.

---

48 David Pilling, 'What is Nigeria's government for?', *Financial Times*, 31 January 2022.

The Godfather Rules OK

*Political power is not going to be served in a restaurant . . .
not served in [sic] a la carte. It is what we are doing. It is
being determined to do it at all cost. Fight for it! Grab it!
Snatch it! And run with it!*

– Bọ́lá Ahmed Tinúbú

*I will challenge this rascality for the future of the country.
This is not the end but the beginning of the journey for the
birth of a new Nigeria.*

– Peter Obi

The previous chapter detailed the many sins of Bọ́lá
Ahmed Tinúbú but omitted his 1993 indictment in the
United States for 'narcotics trafficking and money laundering', for which he forfeited US$460,000. In other
words, as of 29 May 2023, Nigeria's president is a
drug-dealing thug (as predicted some years ago by somebody who should have known), whose name, age and
place of birth are all in doubt, which neatly tells us
everything we need to know about the condition of a
country now entering its endgame, even as all too many
Nigerians pray to Allah/Ancestors/God (we are promis-
cuous in these matters) to touch the heart of the latest
scoundrel, who will then miraculously do the needful
and earn the country its proper place in the comity of

nations – or something to that effect.[1] Whatever the case, he has surely earned himself the Godfather title. Not even Don Corleone in the Hollywood version – whose name, age and place of birth were *not* in doubt – could make his youngest son a 'senator or even governor' because 'there just wasn't enough time' to transition to respectability. In keeping with the logic of the script, most people believe that Tinúbú of the misnamed All Progressives Congress (APC) bullied and bribed his way through (as in, 'my father assured him that either his brains or his signature will be on the contract,' in the words of Michael Corleone), thereby rendering him illegitimate in the eyes of even the 25 million of the eligible 87 million who bothered to turn out, the lowest percentage of any election since 1999. The fact that the shabby exercise blew US$1.8bn when India, with six times our population, spent just US$470mn on its own elections is the measure of our corruption, epitomised by the president himself.[2]

But even for the many on Tinúbú's extensive payroll – including former crusading journalists and human rights advocates, along with a well-regarded writer – the real winner was Peter Obi of the Labour Party (LP), irrespective of the fact that the misnamed Independent National Electoral Commission (INEC) placed him third behind Atiku Abubakar of the Peoples Democratic Party, whose

---

1 'DRUG BARONS May Determine Nigeria's Future', was the perspicacious 1990 cover of the defunct *Newbreed* magazine currently trending on social media. The quote was directly from Fidelis Oyakhilome, head of the National Drug Law Enforcement Agency from 1988 to 1991.

2 Further comparisons: Brazil, with a roughly similar population, spent US$450mn, and Indonesia, more populous by almost a third, spent US$292mn.

own kleptocratic tendencies are also detailed in the previous chapter.[3] The pity of it is that the 25 February presidential election was supposed to be the freest and fairest ever conducted since the return of what passes for democracy. At a Chatham House meeting the previous month, Mahmood Yakubu, the INEC chair, assured the audience that only an act of Allah/Ancestors/God could prevent the Bimodal Voter Accreditation System (BVAS) from performing optimally: 'Each and every machine has been tested and confirmed functional. For the last two weeks, our officials were in the 36 states of the federation testing these machines, and the functionality is simply encouraging.' As for 'glitches': 'There is always a back up. We have … technical support that will fix the machines in the unlikely event of any glitches.'[4] And then it turned out that there were indeed glitches but only for the presidential election, not the concurrent national assembly election.

So why did it work for one but not the other? At a press conference a week later, Yakubu blamed 'logistics, election technology, behaviour of some election personnel at different levels, attitude of some party agents and supporters'; promised that 'the Commission has intensified the review of the technology to ensure that glitches experienced, particularly with the upload of results are rectified'; and claimed to be confident, going forward, that 'the system will run optimally' but without actually saying what the problem was in the first place. Then it transpired that the

---

3   According to INEC, BAT garnered 8,794,726 votes to Atiku's 6,984,520 and Obi's 6,101,533. The fourth presidential candidate, Rabiu Kwankwaso of the New Nigeria Peoples Party, garnered 1,496,687 votes.

4   Sodiq Omolaoye, '2023: We're ready, INEC chair, Yakubu insists at Chatham House', *Guardian*, 18 January 2023.

real purpose of the BVAS was merely to verify the identities of the voters; it was not meant to upload the results automatically in real time to INEC's Results Viewing Portal (IReV), as most people assumed. On the contrary, the results themselves were to be manually recorded by the presiding officer in the presence of the party agents before they were transferred to IReV, which was where the mago-mago occurred, as international observers reported, for instance the observers from the European Union:

> According to the findings of EU EOM observers, election day was marked by late deployment and opening while polling procedures were not always followed. Polling staff struggled to complete result forms, which were not posted publicly in most polling units observed. The introduction of the BVAS ... and the IReV ... [was] perceived as an important step to ensure the integrity and credibility of the elections. However, uploading of the results using the BVAS did not work as expected and presidential election result forms started to appear on the portal very late on election day, raising concerns.[5]

Even the outgoing US ambassador, Mary Beth Leonard, issued a statement to the effect that although the people 'demonstrated their dedication to democracy on February 25', there were 'many angry and frustrated Nigerians' for whom 'the electoral process as a whole failed to meet [their] expectations'. It was for this reason that a disappointed Chimamanda Ngozi Adichie, the Nigerian novelist, chastised

---

5   'Elections held on schedule, but lack of transparency and operational failures reduced trust in the process and challenged the right to vote', European Union Election Observation Mission Nigeria, EEAS, 27 February 2023.

US President Joe Biden in an open letter for rushing to congratulate the president-elect, thereby providing 'the sheen of legitimacy to an illegitimate process', even as social media was 'flooded with evidence of irregularities':

> Result sheets were now slowly being uploaded on the INEC portal, and could be viewed by the public. Voters compared their cellphone photos with the uploaded photos and saw alterations: numbers crossed out and rewritten; some originally written in black ink had been rewritten in blue, some blunderingly whited-out with Tipp-Ex. The election had been not only rigged, but done in such a shoddy, shabby manner that it insulted the intelligence of Nigerians. It is ironic that many images of altered result sheets showed votes overwhelmingly being transferred from the Labour Party to the APC.[6]

Subsequently, a team of BBC reporters found hard evidence in the ever-volatile Rivers State, where they examined results' sheets from over 6,000 polling units (out of 6,800) whose websites they were able to access.[7] In general, they discovered that although Tinúbú was declared winner by 'a clear majority', Obi actually 'received [the] most votes in the state by a wide margin': 'We found an increase of just over 106,000 in Mr Tinubu's vote in the official declaration when compared with our polling station tally – almost doubling his total in the state. In contrast, Mr Obi's vote had fallen by over 50,000.' Two local government areas in particular stood out. One was Oyigbo, where the

---

6 Chimamanda Adichie, 'Nigeria's Hollow Democracy', *Atlantic*, 6 April 2023.

7 Chiagozie Nwonwu, Peter Mwai & Karina Igonikon, 'Nigeria election: the mystery of the altered results in disputed poll', BBC, 16 May 2023.

journalists found that Tinúbú's vote 'was six times larger in the officially announced results compared with the BBC's polling station count', while Obi's 'had been cut in half'. The second was in nearby Obio/Akpor, where Tinúbú was supposed to have garnered 80,239 votes but the BBC counted just 17,293, whereas Obi, whose official figure was 3,829, actually won 74,033 of the votes. As it happens, the Oyigbo election was broadcast live on television on 27 February 'in front of a bank of microphones' by one Dr Dickson Ariaga, who claimed to be employed by the Federal College of Education in Omoku. He proceeded to read out the results for each party in alphabetical order, all of which 'matched those on the collation sheet the BBC had obtained' until he came to APC, when, 'instead of saying 2,731 as written on our photograph of the sheet, he read out 16,630'. Similarly, the figures for Obi's LP were changed from 22,289 to 10,784.

And then it turned out that Dr Ariaga was a phantom, a ghost, an apparition, which was fitting enough for an event that was itself a burlesque, a travesty, a mockery. When contacted by the BBC, INEC 'would not give us his details or reach out to him for us'. As for the college, the deputy provost denied all knowledge of the fellow: 'From our records, both from our payroll and from our human resources, there is no such a name in our system and we don't know such a person.' The reporters eventually came across a 'Facebook account for someone in Port Harcourt, whose profile details had the name Dickson Ariaga'. They compared an image from the account to his television pictures using Amazon Rekognition software, which showed a match of 97.2 percent. The man himself refused to respond to messages, but after reaching out to some of his Facebook friends the BBC team finally spoke to someone claiming to be a relative 'who was at first willing to help us but then didn't return our calls'. Meanwhile, INEC's regional spokesperson in Port Harcourt claimed that a 'gross shortage of time and personnel' meant that 'they had needed to take on some people without verifying their identity documents', but that if indeed he misrepresented himself as a lecturer 'then he is dishonest'. INEC headquarters in Abuja 'were unable to comment due to ongoing legal challenges'. As the report concluded, 'This is just one case in one state in southern Nigeria where the evidence points to the results having been manipulated.'

Yakubu himself appeared unmoved by these claims and at 4:10 a.m. on 1 March he announced Tinúbú president-elect, as if anxious to get it done under cover of darkness and exit the scene while most of the country slumbered. Rumours claimed that he had been flown to London ahead of the elections for discussions with the man he had just crowned, even as it was later bruited that the same treatment was accorded the chief justice of the federation (of which more presently), although why everybody needed to go to London to conduct an election in Nigeria perhaps tells us something of the colo-mentality, to use Fẹlá Kútì's phrase. It is to be noted, in any case, that Rishi Sunak, the British prime minister, was just as eager as President Biden to congratulate our wonder boy.

For all that, APC still managed to lose in its candidate's own (supposed) Lagos State to Peter Obi's LP, indication enough of Tinúbú's widespread unpopularity. Obi himself had become the unlikely flag-bearer of the young people who had demonstrated peacefully in the #EndSARS movement in October 2020 until they were mowed down by soldiers, as detailed in the opening chapter. He also happened to be Igbo, which was why the Godfather couldn't allow the LP victory in the 18 March gubernatorial and state assembly elections. What happened on that day was neatly captured in a doctored photo showing Tinúbú and Babájídé Sanwó-Olú, the state governor gunning for a second term, on the back of an okada motorbike taxi speeding off with a ballot box. As it happens, it was based on a real photo of two agbèròs doing just that. The caption was also real: 'Grab it! Snatch it! And run with it!', as Tinúbú had instructed his inner circle at a meeting in London in early December, one of whom approvingly shouted 'Jagaban!' ('Warrior!'). And just two days before the election, his chief agbèrò, Musiliu Akínsànyà, aka MC Oluomo, publicly warned the Igbo (who comprise 40 percent of the population) to stay indoors given that they would invariably vote for their kinsman, as they had done three weeks earlier: 'We have begged them. If they don't want to vote for us, it is not a fight . . . If you don't want to vote for us, sit down at home.' He later claimed that it was just a 'joke'. The police agreed with him – 'Let us take it as a joke, just like he said' – when people wondered why he hadn't been arrested on suspicion of inciting violence. On the day itself, the same police looked the other way while the 'boys' went about their work in groups of a dozen or so, noisily drinking from the apparently endless supply of beer, as I saw for myself in my own middle-class Surùlérè constituency. Reports from the poorer neighbourhoods described Igbo – and even Yorùbá suspected to be such – beaten up for the temerity of simply steeping outside.

After it was all over and Sanwó-Olú's re-election secured, Báyọ̀ Ọnánúgá, Tinúbú's chief media spokesperson (I almost said his deputy agbèrò), issued a warning: 'Let 2023 be the last time of Igbo interference in Lagos politics. Let there be no repeat in 2027. Lagos is like Anambra, Imo, any Nigerian state. It is not No Man's Land, not Federal Capital Territory. It is Yoruba land. Mind your business.' This once respected journalist, who was among those targeted by the military in the bad old days when they annulled elections and judicially murdered Ken Saro-Wiwa, appeared to have forgotten his visit to the Kigali Genocide Memorial in Rwanda in 2018, which he left 'deeply sober', recommending it 'as a must-go place to ethnic Champions . . . harbouring hatred about their fellow human beings . . . Our ethnic identity is determined for us by our maker. So why do we hate a person because he is not a member of our ethnic group?'

In fact, APC was especially spooked by Rhodes-Vivour, LP's gubernatorial candidate, who, although Yorùbá on his father's side, has both an Igbo mother and wife, thereby annulling the ethnic card for those inclined to play it, or so one would have hoped. Instead of which, Ọnánúgá's *TheNEWS*, the weekly magazine he had once used to fight injustice, was now reduced to calling the scion of a distinguished Lagos family 'a tribal bigot and a religious fanatic who is determined to put a knife on the rope that ties us together', without saying what this soft-spoken man was supposed to have done. And here was the 'notorious' Sam Omatseye writing in the *Nation*, the Tinúbú-owned national daily that did sterling service on his behalf, which was why few people bothered to read it:

> Rhodes-Vivour has acted like one who wants to stalk a city in silence, like a predator on the sly. No one can blame him for who he loves to marry, who delivered him at birth, or a riven parenthood. But he has to account whether he exploits either or both to rip a community apart. It's not whether someone split his blood ancestry. It is whether it can spill blood.

The fascistic language employed by Nigeria's 'most decorated columnist' – according to his Twitter handle – and his

ilk to vilify their opponents included calling Rhodes-Vivour
by his Igbo first name, Chinedu ('God is leading'), instead
of the Yorùbá one he is better known by, Gbadébọ ('the
one who brings the crown'), thereby implying that the man
himself was denying his 'other', which he wasn't. He was
also called out for apparently speaking better Igbo than
Yorùbá, that is, not being a 'proper' Ọmọ Èkó (child of
Lagos), but given his background – expensive Lagos boarding school, Massachusetts Institute of Technology – he
probably speaks better English than either Nigerian language, in common with many from his background, as he
acknowledged when he referred to himself as 'an epitome
of Cosmopolitan Lagos'.

One of Rhodes-Vivour's promises was to end the monopoly of Tinúbú's tax-collecting firm, Alpha Beta Consulting,
and with it the 'state capture that focuses on milking the
state for the interest of one man and his family and cronies'. Some believed that this was enough to endanger his
life, and he would claim that his convoy was shot at during
a visit to the suburb of Epe, where he was otherwise
received with much fanfare. The police denied any such
incident ever happened, but there was a precedent. Just
before midday on 27 July 2006, as Tinúbú was coming to
the end of his second term as state governor, Funsho Wil-
liams was killed in his study in an otherwise secure gated
community on Lagos Island. A fifty-eight-year-old engineer
with experience in the state government during the military
era, he had signalled his intention to run for governor on
the platform of the opposition party. A popular figure, his
chances of defeating Tinúbú's anointed successor presaged
those of Rhodes-Vivour sixteen years later. He was found
lying face down in a pool of blood, his hands tied behind
his back, a dagger wrapped in newspaper protruding
from his corpse. The post-mortem confirmed that he died

of 'manual strangulation'. The state government invited detectives from the UK to prove that it had nothing to hide, but by then the crime scene had been hopelessly compromised. A major road was later named after him, arousing even more suspicion.

Fortunately, Rhodes-Vivour survived, but the language from Tinúbú's camp grew increasingly shrill as more and more people openly called for the transfer of power on 29 May to be delayed until the courts had made their judgment. In a television interview, Yusuf Datti Baba-Ahmed, Obi's running mate, cited Section 134 of the Constitution, which states that a candidate must win 25 percent of the votes cast in at least two-thirds of the thirty-six states *and* the Federal Capital Territory, Abuja.[8] Echoing the 1979 election, Tinúbú, like Shagari then, failed to meet this stipulation, which meant that he 'has not satisfied the requirement to be declared president-elect' and therefore 'there is no president-elect for Nigeria now'. For that reason, Baba-Ahmed called on the outgoing President Buhari to 'not hold that inauguration' and the chief justice to 'not participate in unconstitutionality', and he added: 'It is extreme and I'm saying it. It was more extreme for Yakubu to issue that certificate. It was reckless.'

Tinúbú's cheerleaders promptly went ballistic. Here was Ọnánúgá openly threatening 'those sons of bitches tweeting the Hashtags #TinubuTheDrugDealer #TinubuForPrison' but whose 'days are numbered'; here was Fẹ́mi Fani-Káyọ̀dé calling Obi 'a master terrorist' leading an 'army of ignorant, fascist, violent, uncouth, frustrated, garrulous, racist, bigoted, misguided, radical, brash and rebellious supporters' (how do we know he went to Oxford University?); and here, alas, was Wọlé Ṣóyínká, our revered Nobel

8 'Politics Today', Channels Television, 22 March 2023.

laureate, accusing Yusuf Datti of 'fascistic language' that is 'not acceptable'. Following widespread criticism of his choice of language, Ṣóyínká hit back with typical acerbity by reiterating the offensive word even as he proposed a one-on-one debate on the same station where the vice-presidential hopeful had made his position clear (the latter declined):

> It would appear that a record discharge of toxic sludge from our notorious smut factory is currently clogging the streets and sewers of the Republic of Liars. It goes to prove the point that provoked the avalanche EXACTLY! The seeds of incipient fascism in the political arena have evidently matured. A climate of fear is being generated. The refusal to entertain corrective criticism, even differing perspectives of the same position has become a badge of honour and certificate of commitment.[9]

This was the same Ṣóyínká who held up a radio station at gunpoint following the contested 1965 elections that Fani-Káyọdé's father, Rẹ̀mí, boasted were rigged in order to deliver the 'correct' result (for which he was charged but acquitted on a technicality); the same Ṣóyínká who – however misguidedly – travelled to the east to confer with Ojukwu to try and prevent the civil war which he now seems to be courting. But what we are witnessing is the dying old – literally and metaphorically – attempting to prevent the birth of the new, as represented in the person of the forty-year-old Rhodes-Vivour with his 'dual heritage', and in the more than 70 percent of voters under the age of thirty-five for whom he is Nigerian before he is Chinedu or Gbadébọ̀, a phenomenon that the real 'tribal bigots' waxed

---

9   Wole Soyinka, 'Fascism on Course', *Premium Times*, 7 April 2023.

hysterical over. The youths want change and they want it now because there is no more time left; as 'the shitty little diva' (that is, Chimamanda Ngozi Adichie) observed in her 'shitty little submission' to President Biden (as Fani-Káyòdé' would have it, his elevated education notwithstanding), 'rage is brewing, especially among young people. The discontent, the despair, the tension in the air have not been this palpable in years.'[10]

To worsen matters, this rage is unnecessarily compounded by the constitutional provision which allows the election tribunal 180 days to deliver its judgment, and a further 60 days for the Supreme Court to consider any appeals. This means that Tinúbú was already sworn into office before the tribunal even finished its deliberations, beginning with his failure to achieve the required number of votes in the Federal Capital Territory. In a letter to INEC, Dr Olisa Agbakoba, SAN, a former president of the Nigerian Bar Association, agreed that the relevant section of the constitution might be construed as ambiguous: 'Does this mean that the Federal Capital Territory, Abuja is incorporated in the 24 States? Or . . . does it mean that the presidential candidate must also score not less than one-quarter of the votes cast at the election at the Federal Capital Territory, Abuja?' Nevertheless, in a subsequent TV interview, he pointed out that it is a purely legislative matter, easily dealt with in a week, and that simply because the law allows for six months doesn't mean that the courts must adhere to that timeframe, especially in a case where 'the polity is overheated'. He also pointed out that 'there is a certain unfairness for a petitioner to challenge a president-elect who goes on to get inaugurated'. He might have added that

---

10   Adichie, 'Nigeria's Hollow Democracy'. Fani-Káyòdé' issued his scatological diatribe on Twitter.

the de facto president automatically has much greater power to influence events, the more so in a country such as ours.

However, Agbakoba did concede that resolving election malpractice charges will be altogether more challenging, not least given INEC's foot-dragging over releasing the relevant materials, the otherwise supposedly neutral umpire itself blatantly acting as an interested party. It should be noted, by comparison, that Turkey took just one day to announce the result of its first inconclusive presidential election without anybody disputing the result, and this under the twenty-year reign of a 'strongman' who isn't accused of bribing polling officials, presumably because he and they have too much respect for their country as a coherent entity, a respect they demonstrated again when they held a run-off that was also concluded in one day. Meanwhile, we continue to muddy the waters back home.

In the meantime, INEC itself pressed ahead with its inauguration programme, which kicked off on 18 March with a world press conference by the secretary to the government of the federation. This was followed on 23 March by a regimental dinner in honour of the outgoing president Buhari, on the occasion of which he invested Tinúbú with the nation's highest honour, Grand Commander in the Order of the Federal Republic, and his running mate, Kassim Shettima (of whom more presently), with the second-highest, Grand Commander in the Order of the Niger. But the truly surreal event occurred two days before the actual handover when Uhuru M. Kenyatta, a former president of Kenya who headed the African Union monitoring group for the elections, delivered an inauguration lecture titled 'Deepening Democracy for Integration and Development'. Perhaps the title was chosen when Yakubu was giving his lecture at

Chatham House, but this noble intention will be made all the more difficult to adhere to by the staggering amount of money that is about to be looted by departing public officers in a country already up to its eyeballs in debt, having already paid themselves more than their 'developed' counterparts.

According to the Revenue Mobilization and Fiscal Allocation Commission, the severance package for Buhari, his vice president, the state governors and others on leaving office was a whooping ₦63.45bn. All are entitled to a one-off payment of 300 percent of their annual salary, with some state governors also receiving 100 percent of their annual basic salary for life, not to mention the various emoluments certain governors approved for themselves through their state legislatures. Tinúbú, for instance, as a former governor of Lagos was entitled to two houses in Lagos and Abuja, respectively, six brand new cars replaced every three years, a furniture allowance of 300 percent of his annual salary to be paid every two years, and a ₦2.5mn monthly pension. This remains the case even for governors who move to the senate after their tenure, where they also collect a handsome salary. Meanwhile, some of these same governors refused to implement the ₦30,000 minimum wage law, perhaps because there was nothing left in their respective states' coffers to pay for it. According to the World Bank Macro Poverty Outlook for Nigeria, last year the country used 96.3 percent of revenue generated to service its debt, currently standing at ₦68.95tn, a 447 percent increase from the ₦12.6tn. the outgoing administration inherited when it entered office in 2015.

Why anybody would want to take over a country in such a mess is an open question, but so it was that Tinúbú was inaugurated after a strict warning from the chief of defence staff for everyone to stay at home: 'If you don't have any business in and around Eagle Square on 29 May, stay away, otherwise the consequences will be severe.' In his departing speech, Buhari congratulated himself on many accomplishments that were clearly delusional, for instance that he had doubled our infrastructure (nobody else noticed) and birthed a new national airline. Indeed, the latter exemplifies everything that is clownish about the country. What we saw was a single aircraft in the new Nigeria Air colours on the tarmac at Nnamdi Azikiwe International Airport; the plane turned out to belong to Ethiopian Airways and was returned the following day. It was no less of an illusion than deepening the democracy Kenyatta had come to praise him for. In the outgoing incumbent's own deluded words:

> To ensure that our democracy remains resilient and our elected representatives remain accountable to the people, I am leaving behind an electoral process which guarantees that votes count, results are credible, elections are fair and transparent and the influence of money in politics reduced to the barest minimum. And Nigerians can elect leaders of their choice.
>
> We are already seeing the outcome of this process as it provided an even playing field where persons without any political God-Father or access to money defeated other well-resourced candidates.[11]

The inauguration itself was a subdued affair. Tinúbú, who is known to be in poor health and was forever jetting off for medical treatment at the American Hospital of Paris, Neuilly-sur-Seine, didn't slur his words and actually

---

11 'Farewell Speech by His Excellency President Muhammadu Buhari', The State House, Abuja, 28 May 2023.

managed to stand up for his fifteen-minute speech, although when he was leaving the stage he looked confused and had to be chaperoned in the right direction. In the speech itself, he noted the 'surprise of many but not to ourselves' in the election outcome and was pleased that 'we have more firmly established this land as a democracy in both word and deed.'[12] The 'peaceful transition from one government to another is now our political tradition', for which 'we lift high this torch so that it might shine on every household and in every heart that calls itself Nigerian.' He alluded to 'compassion', 'brotherhood' and 'peace' while promising to 'govern on your behalf but never rule over you': 'We shall consult and dialogue but never dictate. We shall reach out to all but never put down a single person for holding views contrary to our own.' In this 'vein', he sought permission to make 'a few comments regarding the election that brought us to this juncture'. Noting that it 'was a hard-fought contest . . . also fairly won', he claimed that since 'the advent of the Fourth Republic, Nigeria has not held an election of better quality', reflecting as it did 'the will of the people'. As for the ongoing legal cases, he said it was the right of the aggrieved parties to seek 'legal redress', which he fully supported because that is 'the essence of the rule of law'. For himself, 'political coloration has faded away' and 'all I see are Nigerians,' whereupon he waxed lyrical:

> Whether from the winding creeks of the Niger Delta, the vastness of the northern savannah, the boardrooms of Lagos, the bustling capital of Abuja, or the busy markets of Onitsha, you are all my people. As your president, I shall

---

12 'First Inaugural Address by President Bola Ahmed Tinubu', The State House, Abuja, 29 May 2023.

serve with prejudice toward none but compassion and amity towards all.

But what was especially dispiriting in all of this was the way the ethnic card was deployed to get Tinúbú there, which is the final proof that it was all about one elderly man's suffocating sense of entitlement – 'it's my turn' – to achieve such a shoddy 'victory', as even his cheerleaders seem to have realised, which is why they have since toned down the rhetoric. As in the civil war half a century ago that we seem intent on repeating, the Yorùbá have once again teamed up with the Hausa-Fulani, in the process squandering the people's opportunity to choose an Igbo president and thereby bring closure to the national wound. Not that the youths who overwhelmingly supported the sixty-one-year-old Obi considered him a saint. They are not so naive; they know very well the country that birthed them, to borrow the language of Sam Omatseye. Nobody gets to be a two-term governor in the murky arena of Nigerian politics without soiling their hands, and the Panama Papers revealed that, while governor, Obi failed to declare the offshore company he registered in the British Virgin Islands to the Code of Conduct Bureau, the agency that deals with the issues of corruption, conflict of interest and abuse of office by public servants. He said he was unaware that the law expected him to declare assets or companies he jointly owned with his family members. Obi has also admitted to using offshore companies to avoid paying tax; as he put it: 'I am sure you too will not like to pay inheritance tax if you can avoid it.'[13] That aside, he had

---

13 Taiwo Hassan Adebayo, 'PANDORA PAPERS: Inside Peter Obi's secret business – and how he broke the law', *Premium Times*, 4 October 2021.

a reputation for probity in the running of the state's affairs when he was governor, although that wasn't too difficult given the fellow he took over from. For the first time, teachers and pensioners were paid as and when due; he invested heavily in infrastructure while nonetheless managing to leave Anambra the least indebted state in the country. A former banker, he also started a sub-sovereign wealth fund, the first of its kind in sub-Saharan Africa.

What he also has going for him is his humble demeanour, as I once saw for myself when we were introduced by a mutual friend in the lobby of an Abuja hotel shortly after he had left office. Soft-spoken and courteous even to someone he was meeting for the first time, he is known to carry his own bag and sit in the economy section, the better to relate to his fellow citizens. In other words, he is the antithesis of the brash, loud, swaggering politician who needs to be constantly reassured that he is, indeed, a Big Man (and it is mostly men, Nigeria having one the lowest percentages of women elected representatives in the world, behind even the Islamic Republic of Iran). More ominously for Tinúbú, Obi also has form when it comes to election tribunals. It took him nearly three years to win his mandate following the 2003 gubernatorial contest. Nine months later, he was impeached by the state house of assembly, which he successfully challenged and was reinstated. He was forced to leave office once again following the 2007 elections but returned to the courts contending that the four-year term to which he was elected in 2003 only began when he actually took office in 2006. One year later, the Supreme Court agreed with him. He won a second term in a by-election in 2010.

So it looked as if everything now rested in the hands of the judiciary, but the signs were not good. Even before he assumed office, Tinúbú spoke about the need to pay attention to the 'welfare' of the country's judges: 'You don't expect your judges to live in squalor, to operate in squalor and dispense justice in squalor. This is part of the changes that are necessary. We must fight corruption but we must definitely look at the other side of the coin.' Not long afterwards, it was rumoured that Tinúbú tasked the re-elected Lagos State governor to come up with ₦100bn to bribe judges, whereupon his boy dutifully signed ₦135bn in bonds, ostensibly to upgrade thirty-three schools in the slum area of Ajegunle.[14] For his part, the chief justice of the federation, Olúkáyòdé Ariwoọlá, was quick to declare that his hands 'are clean' and that judges handling presidential petitions 'must show no bias and do justice to restore confidence in the judiciary'. However, as with the INEC chairman, Ariwoọlá, too, was rumoured to have visited Tinúbú in London after the justice was caught on film at the Lagos airport in clumsy disguise aboard a wheelchair he doesn't otherwise need. Indeed, the courts might have already set a precedent in Tinúbú's case. Just three days before the inauguration, the court of appeal ruled in favour of Vice President–elect Kassim Shettima, who was held to have simultaneously stood for a second term in the senate, in contravention of Section 35 of the Constitution. Shettima himself won many plaudits as governor of Borno State from 2011 to 2019, when he moved to the senate, and he may yet become president if his boss's health is as bad as rumour has it, which would mean power returning to the Hausa-Fulani, but that is beside the point at this late stage.

Half a year after the election, in October 2023, a ruling by the country's highest court duly upheld the results. As I

---

14 'Sanwo-Olu signs N135 bn. bonds for LASG to upgrade 33 Ajegunle schools', *Supreme Magazine*, 24 May 2023.

argued in the preface, Nigeria has no future as presently constituted, and this aside from the failure of Atiku and Obi's legal challenges, which might even be a distraction from the real work at hand. We have to restructure if we are to find our way out of this morass in which a few choose to drink champagne and the many are denied clean drinking water, inequality so blatant that the recently elected governor of Zamfara State, Dauda Lawal, a former banker, supposedly declared he had assets of ₦9tn, although his handlers were quick to denounce his having made such a statement as a 'ridiculous and fabricated lie' that was 'created and pushed in social media . . . by mischief makers bent on distracting the new government', but then they would say so. Moreover, the vast majority of people will believe it because it is true in an existential sense, the sense in which it ought to be true because this is Nigeria. And so it is that we seem intent on doing violently what we have refused to do peacefully. In any case, the future lies in the hands of the youths, if only they can seize it; it certainly does not lie in the small minority of old men whom the youths themselves enable out of so-called 'tradition', where respect for the 'elders' is supposedly sacred, no matter how much money they steal or how many little girls they defile, because, after all, Allah/Ancestors/God permits it. Court judgment or not, this government is illegitimate, as the government itself well knows. And now, as we enter uncharted territory, we can expect a much greater escalation in civil disobedience based on the #EndSARS movement, along with a matching escalation in banditry, kidnapping and Islamic fundamentalism as the country slowly disintegrates. The politicians know perfectly well that this fiction called Nigeria cannot survive their depredations that are enabled by the very fact that nobody ever owed allegiance to someone else's abstraction that we have refused to take responsibility for. This is why they buy houses in Dubai and educate their children in the UK, where they also go when they have a headache, possibly to be treated by a Nigerian doctor trained at some expense at home before fleeing to saner climes.